Visible Learning: Feedback

Feedback is arguably the most critical and powerful aspect of teaching and learning. Yet, there remains a paradox: why is feedback so powerful and why is it so variable? It is this paradox which *Visible Learning: Feedback* aims to unravel and resolve.

Combining research excellence, theory and vast teaching expertise, this book covers the principles and practicalities of feedback, including:

- the variability of feedback,
- the importance of surface, deep and transfer contexts,
- student to teacher feedback,
- peer to peer feedback,
- the power of within lesson feedback and manageable post-lesson feedback.

With numerous case studies, examples and engaging anecdotes woven throughout, the authors also shed light on what creates an effective feedback culture and provide the teaching and learning structures which give the best possible framework for feedback.

Visible Learning: Feedback brings together two internationally known educators and merges Hattie's world-famous research expertise with Clarke's vast experience of classroom practice and application, making this book an essential resource for teachers in any setting, phase or country.

John Hattie is Laureate Professor at the University of Melbourne, Australia and chair of the Australian Institute for Teaching and School Leadership. He is the author of the globally bestselling Visible Learning series of books and co-edited with Eric Anderman the original International Guide to Student Achievement published in 2013.

Shirley Clarke is an internationally known expert on the practical application of the principles of formative assessment. Her career includes teaching, test writing, lecturing for 10 years at the Institute of Education, University of London and directing numerous national research projects. Her bestselling books have made assessment practice relevant and accessible.

Visible Learning: Feedback

John Hattie and Shirley Clarke

 Routledge
Taylor & Francis Group

LONDON AND NEW YORK

First published 2019
by Routledge
2 Park Square, Milton Park, Abingdon, Oxon OX14 4RN

and by Routledge
711 Third Avenue, New York, NY 10017

Routledge is an imprint of the Taylor & Francis Group, an informa business

© 2019 John Hattie and Shirley Clarke

British Library Cataloguing in Publication Data
A catalogue record for this book is available from the British Library

Library of Congress Cataloging in Publication Data
A catalog record for this book has been requested

ISBN: 978-1-138-59988-8 (hbk)
ISBN: 978-1-138-59989-5 (pbk)
ISBN: 978-0-429-48548-0 (ebk)

Typeset in Bembo and Helvetica Neue
by Apex CoVantage, LLC

Table of Contents

List of figures

Introduction

John Hattie

John Hattie began his career as a teacher in primary and secondary schools, before moving into academia. His PhD is in measurement and statistics, and he has spent his career using these methods to better address educational questions. He has worked at the Universities of New England, Western Australia, North Carolina, Auckland and now Melbourne.

John is Laureate Professor at the University of Melbourne and co-director of the Science of Learning Research Centre. He is chair of the Australian Institute for Teachers and School Leaders, honorary professor at the University Durham and Auckland. He is past-president of the International Test Commission and associate editor of the *British Journal of Educational Psychology and Nature: Science of Learning* and serves on the board of 28 journals.

He has supervised 200 thesis students to completion (and is most proud of this) and published and presented over 1,000 papers. His hobby is collecting meta-analyses, aiming to evaluate the relative impact of various interventions. This led to Visible Learning (2009) and now 14 related books, translations into 24 languages, workshops around the world and a mission to more deeply understand the underlying story as to the most important influences.

In September 2001, he met Shirley Clarke in Chester, UK and was so impressed with her skills at translating research into teacher friendly books, he asked to work with her – which has led to a best-seller about formative assessment in New Zealand. He has gained from the critiques of his work by Shirley that have sharpened claims and arguments, leading to this book.

Shirley Clarke

Shirley Clarke is an internationally known expert in formative assessment. She works with teams of teachers every year evaluating formative assessment strategies linked with research findings to evolve the practical application of formative assessment. Her many publications and presentations have enabled teachers across the world to have access to research and practical tried and tested strategies. Her work has had a major influence on practice in schools across the UK and beyond.

A former primary teacher in England, she went on to become a mathematics adviser, a test writer and then an academic at the Institute of Education, University College London, during which time she conducted a number of national research projects looking at the impact of testing on teachers and students. She was awarded an honorary doctorate in 2007.

Her publications, with a number of translations, are worldwide best sellers in schools because they combine research with practice in a tried and tested, accessible way. She has added to the support for teachers by capturing video of teachers in action, and now has 140 high quality clips on her website video platform (www.shirleyclarke-education.org). Seeing formative assessment in action by excellent teachers is a powerful way of communicating its impact and use.

In 2001 a New Zealand version of Shirley's book *Unlocking Formative Assessment* was published, which was the beginning of the liaison with John Hattie, culminating in this book, linking *Visible Learning* with research findings, practical strategies and examples of excellent practice of feedback.

Acknowledgments

Co-writing a book 17,000 kilometers apart is fun – it heightens the writing. It leads to continual debates and it makes the rare face to face meetings (dinners) all the more fun. This book has had a long gestation – we both considered feedback as a critical determiner for enhancing student and teacher learning many eons ago. But the variability was so great. How come about one third of feedback is negative and the same feedback in some situations is powerful but in others detracts? We both explored these notions – in the research, in the lab and in the classroom. We developed models and theories, we moved from research to practice and practice back to theory. So many critiqued, questioned, offered ideas and advice. It took 15 years of collaboration before we both felt confident we were ready to put pen to paper.

I thank my colleagues at the various universities I have worked at, my current PhD students, my *Visible Learning* partners around the world (*Cognition*, Corwin; *Challenging Learning*, Osiris, Bazalt, Onderwijs-Advies) and the many who email with constructive critique. In particular, Luke Mandouit, Cam Brookes and Mark Gan have sharpened these ideas.

I have been with Janet over 30 years and she remains my best critic, provider of feedback and love of my life. Her greatest skills include patience, love, fortitude and good fun and she is the best thing that ever happened to me – followed by my family: Joel, Kat, Kyle, Jess, Kieran, Alesha, Edna, Patterson and grandchild Emma.

John Hattie

I thank those colleagues from way back when who gave me opportunities to conduct national research projects at the Institute of Education in London and saw the value of combining research with practice, (a rare thing in the nineties) especially Caroline Gipps, Peter Mortimore, Denis Lawton and Barbara MacGilchrist. Chas Knight, the Hodder editor of all my books so far, deserves special thanks, as his excellence and understanding of what I wanted to achieve played a great part in their accessibility and popularity.

In my ongoing work with many schools and teams of teachers trialling formative assessment strategies, I wish to thank Seamus Gibbons and Gary Wilkie who have worked with me from young teachers to school leaders of excellent schools and along the way have contributed invaluable insights about the real world of formative assessment in action, also Kim Zeidler from the University of East Kentucky who purchased 1000 copies of my latest book for her students, so convinced was she of the power of formative assessment, and invited me to work with teachers there. The subsequent knowledge gained about the nitty gritty of the American school widened my horizons, as well as the two years living in Wisconsin working with educators.

Thanks go to all the educators across the world who agreed to contribute excellent examples of feedback in action to this book. These examples of practice bring the research to life and make it more likely that many other teachers will be able to put theory into practice.

A special thanks to Dylan Wiliam, the guru of formative assessment, who kindly made helpful suggestions for the book.

My husband, John, always gives enthusiastic support to my work and his attention to detail in providing administrative support as well as love and patience is greatly appreciated.

Most of all I have to thank John Hattie for the great privilege of being asked to co-author a book with him. It has been an honor to be collaborating with one of the greatest educators of our time, and his desire to combine both our skills has confirmed my long-standing belief that it is when research meets classroom practice that you get the greatest impact – on teaching, on learning, on future lives.

We thank our Routledge team, especially Bruce Roberts, who has overseen many of the *VL* books, ensuring they are well edited and presented and he has become a long-time friend.

Shirley Clarke

Note

Throughout this book we have included multiple practical examples. Although the arguments put forward are quite generic and applicable to all phases of education, we had to decide how to make the content as accessible as possible for all readers. Thus there are more elementary examples than middle or high school, so that readers do not need advanced subject specific knowledge in order to fully understand those arguments.

Effect sizes

John Hattie's Visible Learning is based on his ongoing synthesis of meta-analyses about the effects of the various influences on learning. Each influence on learning has a carefully calculated effect size, with 0.4 as the mean across over 250 influences. The higher the effect size, the greater the positive influence and the lower the effect size, the smaller.

CHAPTER

1

What is feedback?

This chapter summarizes the key points about the nature and development of feedback thinking by educators and academics, laying the foundation for the related issues to be explored throughout the rest of this book. The subsequent chapters are closely tied to the life of a teacher and a student in the day to day structure of lessons, as outlined in the introduction: culture, learning strategies, in lesson feedback and post-lesson feedback. Practical examples, wherever possible, will bring the findings to life.

We have asked thousands of teachers to answer the following question in a short sentence: What do you mean by feedback? These are typical of the ten main explanations:

> Comments – give comments on the way you are doing something
> Clarification – answering student questions in class
> Criticism – when you are given constructive criticism
> Confirmation – when you are told you are doing it right
> Content development – asking about the comment
> Constructive reflection – giving someone positive and constructive reflections on their work
> Correction – showing what you did right or wrong, which helps you
> Cons and pros – someone telling the pros and cons about your work
> Commentary – they comment on my work
> Criterion – relative to a standard

We have also asked as many students the same question, and by far the top explanation of their list is: feedback helps me know where to go next. Oftentimes when feedback is more about the above ten Cs, the students will claim that they did not receive any feedback. Some direction, some 'where to next?' feedback based on the ten Cs, however, is probably more powerful, as it helps defend the reasons for moving forward. A major focus in this book is ensuring there is 'where to next?' feedback provided.

Some history . . . marking and grading

Not very long ago the word 'feedback' was rarely used. In the US, the term 'grading' covered what was then, and still often now, is assumed to be the most conventional way of giving some kind of response to students about their work or learning. In the UK and other countries, the term 'marking' was used to describe grades, comments or both. The feedback in this form was mainly summative and from teacher to student only. That isn't to say that formative, oral, immediate, student to teacher and student to student feedback wasn't taking place, but it had not been highlighted for its significance.

Marking and grading had come under fire in various studies. Ruth Butler's (1988) famous study, for instance, in which students were given either: a) grades, b) comment only or c) grades and comments found that those in the comment only groups had greater gains in progress (measured by test results) than the other two groups. Wherever positive comments accompanied grades, interviews with students revealed that they ignored those comments in favor of the grade and what it was telling them about their performance. They added that the positive comments were the teacher's way of cheering them up. Grades encourage students to develop ego-related mindsets rather than task-related mindsets. Grades often tell the student 'the work is over'. We must not confuse grading with feedback.

As comment only feedback became more common, the next step was to make sure it was specific enough to make a difference. The Office for Standards in Education (Ofsted) (the schools' inspection service) wrote to schools in England in 1996:

> Marking is usually contentious but often fails to offer guidance on how work can be improved. In a significant minority of cases, marking reinforces underachievement and under expectation by being too generous or unfocused.

The essential message is that the most valuable feedback focuses on helping the student improve. If the comments do not provide 'where to next' or 'how to improve this work' information then grades might be the only worthwhile indicator; but if grades are given with no other information, this might not lead to defensible interpretation as to current or future improvements.

Teachers were generally giving grades, comments, or both, to students *after* lessons, and these were seen as the most important and expected form of feedback. It was also discovered that most comments, unless they required a student response, were often ignored by students if the feedback comments were given out with no time allocated for students to read the comments, no chance to use them to improve, or where they were illegible or hard to understand (e.g. Clarke, 2001).

Feedback: timing

Nuthall and Alton-Lee (1997) found that all students, regardless of their level of achievement, typically need to be exposed to any new learning at least three to five times before it has a high probability of being learned.

> Our data does not support the notion that lower achievers need more instruction. The critical requirement is that all students get access to comparable opportunities.
>
> *(Nuthall & Alton-Lee, 1997)*

During the multiple opportunities for learning and engagement, teachers need to provide feedback to refine the student's understanding of the content. Teachers need to plan for students' misconceptions to be identified, explored and challenged, to make transparent the links with their prior experiences and to provide multiple opportunities and scaffolding to make those links with new information: the essence of effective feedback. Nuthall is quite emphatic that students do not need merely repeated trials at tasks – there must be punctuating feedback. Doing the same thing (making the same errors) repeatedly leads to overlearning the wrong things. Neither should students have simply more experience of the same teaching, but instead a variety of experiences and feedback over three to five interactions.

Feedback: what matters

Hattie and Timperley (2007) defined feedback as relating to actions or information provided by an agent (e.g. teacher, peer, book, parent, internet, experience) that provides information regarding aspects of one's performance or understanding.

Feedback is information about the task that fills a gap between what is understood and what is aimed to be understood. It can lead to increased effort, motivation or engagement to reduce the discrepancy between the current status and the goal; it can lead to alternative strategies to understand the material; it can confirm for the student that they are correct or incorrect, or how far they have reached the goal; it can indicate that more information is available or needed; it can point to directions that the students could pursue; and finally it can lead to restructuring understandings. Royce Sadler (1989) set the scene in his seminal paper by establishing the concept that feedback is information that 'closes the gap' between where a student is and where the student needs to be:

> The learner has to a) possess a concept of the standard (or goal or reference level) being aimed for, b) compare the actual (or current) level of performance with the standard, and c) engage in appropriate action which leads to some closure of the gap.

Once 'feedback' entered the teaching vocabulary, the power of verbal, in-lesson feedback between all parties and the place and quantity of post-lesson feedback became, and remains, a key focus. The research findings made the scope of feedback something that could not be ignored.

Rather than general, meaningless comments as feedback to the student (e.g. 'Try harder'), Terry Crooks revealed the most effective feedback content (2001):

> The greatest motivational benefits will come from focusing feedback on:
>
> - the qualities of the child's work, and not on comparison with other children,
> - specific ways in which the child's work could be improved,
> - improvements that the child has made compared to his or her earlier work.

All this needs to be undertaken in a climate of high trust and reduced anxiety. The issue of the attention paid to children's self-efficacy and self-esteem and the use of external rewards and other forms of extrinsic motivation was linked with types of feedback:

> Feedback is most effective when goals are specific and challenging but when task complexity is low. Giving praise for completing a task appears to be ineffective. Feedback is more effective when there are perceived low rather than high levels of threat to self-esteem.
>
> *(Kluger & DeNisi, 1996)*

Getting underneath student understanding, finding out what they really think, is the starting point of all feedback, from whichever direction, because only then can the feedback be appropriately constructed to provide advice:

> When I completed the first synthesis of 134 meta analyses of all possible influences on achievement (Hattie, 1992), it soon became clear that feedback was among the most positive influences on achievement . . . The mistake I was making was seeing feedback as something teachers provided to students. I discovered that feedback is most powerful when it is from the student to the teacher. What they know, what they understand, where they make errors, when they have misconceptions, when they are not engaged – then teaching and learning

can be synchronized and powerful. Feedback to teachers makes learning visible.
(Feedback effect size 0.73)

(Hattie, 2012)

Feedback can have many functions: reinforcing success, correcting errors, helping to unravel misconceptions, suggesting specific improvements, giving improvement advice for the future, praising, punishing or rewarding, all with different levels of effectiveness. Who gives the feedback, whether it is task or ego related, and *how and whether it is received and acted upon* are all factors in its effectiveness. This last point is particularly pertinent: more attention needs to be given to whether and how students receive and act upon feedback, as there seems little point in maximizing the amount and nature of feedback given if it is not received or understood. This is why, throughout this book, we emphasize the interpretations that are made by the receiver about the feedback, and how it helps them answer the question 'Where to next?' or 'How could this be improved?'

Feedback thrives on errors and misconceptions. It might seem pointless to receive feedback about 'where to next' if our work is perfect, although in the case of almost all learning, there can always be some improvement and, in any case, knowing where to next in terms of extending one's learning is always valuable. The power of feedback focused on error and misconceptions is further explored in Chapter 3.

Both positive and negative feedback can have beneficial effects on learning. The untangling of these effects depends on the level at which the feedback is aimed and processed and the interactions between the validity of the feedback and the self-efficacy levels of students. In particular, negative feedback is more powerful at the self-level, causing personal evaluation. Both types can be effective when feedback is about the task, but there are differential effects relating to commitment, mastery or performance orientation and self-efficacy.

That students are taught to receive, interpret and use the feedback provided is probably much more important than focusing on how much feedback is provided by the teacher, as feedback given but not heard is of little use. Students, like adults, quickly learn to be selective listeners – feedback often means more investment in improvement, repeating the work and putting in more effort. Feedback can impact our beliefs about our work, our judgments about quality and can have other costs. The art is turning these costs into benefits in terms of deeper, worthwhile and valuable learning.

Finally, feedback needs to be combined with effective teaching and learning strategies to have the greatest impact. Sometimes, re-teaching is more powerful than just providing feedback. Feedback alone is not the magic bullet, as we describe in the following chapters:

- The culture required to best enable effective feedback.
- The types of teaching and learning strategies and techniques which form a structure within which to create effective feedback opportunities.

- Examples and analysis of the different types of in-lesson feedback.
- Examples and analysis of post-lesson feedback including to and from outside school partners.

Having summarized what we know about feedback, it is important that we acknowledge the fundamental problem – while feedback is powerful, it is also among the most variable of influences. The same feedback in one situation might be worthwhile, but in another situation of little value. Indeed, Kluger and DeNisi (1996) noted that one third of feedback was negative in its impact! Understanding this variability is critical, which is why simple claims about feedback are of low value, a problem explored throughout this book.

The following graphic from 'Coaching Teachers in the Power of Feedback' (Figure 1.1), a resource used in a research project in Australia (Brooks, 2017), summarizes the feedback cycle:

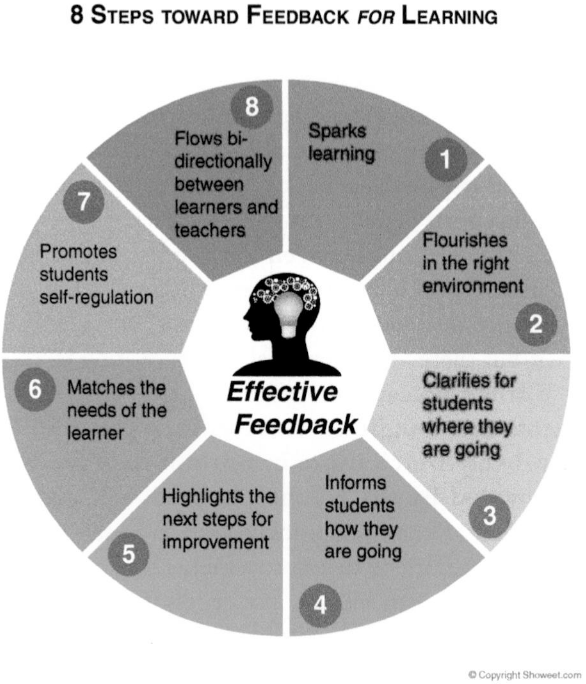

8 STEPS TOWARD FEEDBACK *FOR* LEARNING

© Copyright Showeet.com

Figure 1.1 Toward feedback for learning

Key points

- Feedback is powerful but variable in its impact on learning.
- Grades or comments with no focus on improvement might interfere with learning.
- Students prefer immediate feedback, but delayed feedback can be beneficial.
- Prior knowledge is the starting point for feedback.
- Feedback is about closing the gap between current and desired learning.
- Goals should be specific and challenging, but task complexity low.
- High self-efficacy and trust are needed for feedback to be effective.
- Student to teacher feedback is more important than teacher to student.
- Effective feedback occurs when it is received and acted upon.

2

A feedback culture

This chapter describes a culture in which students and teachers can be best equipped to learn, receive and give feedback. We have considered the elements which have the greatest capacity to make feedback and, therefore, learning effective, whether from teacher to student, student to teacher, student to student, between staff members or involving parents.

The key elements of an effective feedback culture are:

a) That feedback sits within a formative assessment framework.
b) That motivation, curiosity and willingness to learn and deepen current understanding are our aims for all learners (i.e. the skill, will and thrill).
c) That embedded challenge mindsets, mindframes, metacognition and deliberate practice, spaced not massed are effective.
d) That the normalizing and celebration of error is the key to new learning.
e) That equity in learning is maximized through mixed ability grouping.
f) That feedback needs to be task rather than ego related.
g) That we need to privilege the development of a desire to learn and there needs to be an absence of external rewards which act as negative feedback.

a) Feedback sits within a formative assessment framework

Definitions

We use the term 'formative assessment' as it is so firmly established, but we prefer to think of this conceptual framework as 'formative evaluation'. Any test can be interpreted from a formative (where to next?) or a summative (how did I go?) relative to 'Where am I going?' It is the 'when' (during compared to at the end) that distinguishes the two terms. Both are valuable, both need to be based on good information, and both can provide valuable feedback.

Feedback is one of the key ingredients of formative assessment, defined as follows by Black and Wiliam (1998b) in their review of the literature:

The research indicates that improving learning through assessment depends on five, deceptively simple, key factors:

■ the provision of effective feedback to students,
■ the active involvement of students in their own learning,
■ adjusting teaching to take account of the results of assessment,
■ a recognition of the profound influence assessment has on the motivation and self-esteem of students, both of which are crucial influences on learning,
■ the need for students to be able to assess themselves and understand how to improve.

This was further broken down to include:

■ sharing learning goals with students,
■ involving students in self-assessment,
■ providing feedback which leads to students recognizing their next steps and how to take them,
■ underpinned by confidence that every student can improve.

The inhibiting factors identified at the time included:

■ a tendency for teachers to assess quantity of work and presentation rather than the quality of learning,
■ greater attention given to marking and grading, much of it tending to lower the self-esteem of students, rather than to provide advice for improvement,
■ a strong emphasis on comparing students with each other which demoralises the less successful learners,
■ information that is not germane to the learning intentions and success criteria of the task,
■ teachers' feedback to students often serves managerial and social purposes rather than helping them to learn more effectively.

(Black & Wiliam, 1998b)

Principles into practice

The practical application of these principles of formative assessment/evaluation has evolved since then, as teachers have experimented with what this means in practice. It is heartening to see, from our experience, how embedded so many of these elements are now (sharing learning intentions and co-constructing success criteria, peer assessment and diagnostic feedback), but equally depressing to see, despite continuing evidence to the contrary, how many elements that are not conducive to improving learning still remain (comparisons between students in most secondary schools, the dominance of the overuse of grades, and the use of external rewards which compare students with one another).

By 2006, Wiliam had streamlined the elements of formative assessment thus, taking account of the need for in-class feedback and the power of student to student interaction:

- Clarifying and understanding learning intentions and criteria for success.
- Engineering effective classroom discussions, questions and tasks that elicit evidence of learning.
- Providing feedback that moves learners forward.
- Activating students as teaching and learning resources for each other.
- Activating students as owners of their own learning.

By 2009, *Visible Learning* (Hattie, 2009) was published: a synthesis of over 800 meta-analyses relating to student achievement. An effect size of 0.4 was found to be the average of all 100+ influences, based on many millions of students. The power of formative assessment was revealed, along with effect sizes of the component parts, and explanatory summaries of the studies involved. A sample of the elements indicates their power, and, in the case of ability grouping, its lack of merit:

Feedback	0.73
Knowing learning intentions	0.59
Success criteria	0.59
Classroom discussion	0.82
Teacher/student relationships	0.75
Ability grouping	0.12

If we compare Hattie and Timperley's model of feedback (2007) with Black and Wiliam's model of formative assessment (2009) we see three similar core elements:

Hattie and Timperley (2007)	Black and Wiliam (2009)
Where am I going?	Where the learner is going
How am I going?	Where the learner is right now
Where to next?	How to get there

Both models draw on Sadler's three point 'closing the gap' theory (see Chapter 1), taken from Ramaprasad (1983). There are at least seven possible ways for students to 'close the gap'. Students can:

1. Increase their effort, particularly when the effort leads to tackling more challenging tasks rather than just 'doing more'.

2. Abandon the goals and thus eliminate any gap, and this often leads to non-engagement in the pursuit of further goals.
3. Blur the goals, combining them with so many others that they can pick and choose those goals they attained and ignore the others.
4. Change the standard by setting less challenging goals, accepting performance far below their capabilities as satisfactory. With less challenging goals there is a greater probability of attaining them.
5. Develop effective error detection skills, which lead to their own self-feedback.
6. Seek better strategies or be taught to complete the task.
7. Obtain more information from which they can then problem solve or use their self-regulatory proficiencies.

Although it does not help to reduce the gap, students can also reject the feedback as irrelevant or not informative.

There are multiple ways the teacher can help in closing or reducing the gap, by:

■ providing appropriate challenging and specific goals or learning intentions,
■ clarifying the goals,
■ enhancing commitment to the goals,
■ changing the standard (i.e. choosing easier goals),
■ creating a climate that encourages learning from trial and error,
■ motivating the student to achieve the goal,
■ asking for increased effort,
■ helping students develop self-regulation and error seeking skills,
■ narrowing the range of reasonable hypotheses (sometimes by providing the correct answer and thus allowing students to concentrate on learning the processes and strategies (Sweller, 2016)),
■ providing feedback in terms of more surface information from which to build deeper understandings (e.g. the steps involved in long division, or the definition of photosynthesis) and/or,
■ providing feedback about the self-regulatory aspects of learning, particularly when this information is tied closely to the task (Hattie, Biggs & Purdie, 1996).

By 2014 Clarke's action research teams had evolved the practice of the principles of formative assessment as follows:

■ Teachers believing that all students can improve, knowing that intelligence is expandable, where challenge and improvement is the focus and error is welcomed as heralding new learning, and an understanding of what learning means.

- Increasing motivation and ownership by involving students in planning activities for the topics to be covered.
- Having random talk/learning partners, regularly changing, so that mixed ability is enabled, classroom discussion is a key feature of lessons and students are activated as learning resources for one another.
- Prior knowledge lesson starts and effective questioning throughout lessons, giving teachers the means to live and breathe the 'Ausubel effect' (finding out what the learner already knows . . .).
- The sharing of learning intentions and co-construction of the associated success criteria.
- Analysis of examples of what excellent or good products look like relating to the desired success criteria.
- In-lesson feedback via mid-lesson learning stops and analysis of work in progress.
- The development of effective peer cooperative improvement discussions.
- Feedback in oral or written form focusing on success and specific improvement suggestions.

Feedback, therefore, is a key element of a well-developed set of strategies, beliefs and procedures, each having a major, interlocking influence on the other. Without effective learning partners, for instance, students are in no position to carry out effective cooperative feedback or to be regularly used as learning resources for one another. Without a mindset that permits a healthy discussion of errors and mistakes and high self-efficacy, students are unlikely to challenge themselves or see error as exciting. Without clear learning intentions and success criteria, the focus of feedback, from any direction, is likely to be more general, less specific, less helpful in celebrating success and suggesting improvement. We would be unlikely to want to engage in any activity if we did not know its purpose or play a game, for instance, if we did not know the criteria for success. When students know what success means they are more likely to be more committed players in working through the challenges of their learning.

b) The skill, will and thrill

Learning is the outcome of the processes of moving from surface to deep to transfer. Only with this journey will students be able to go beyond the information given to being able to learn, relate the ideas to other ideas, and therefore transfer effectively on their own: knowing much, then using this knowledge in the exploration of relations, applying and extending to other ideas and contexts, and being able to know what to do when one doesn't know what to do. Cultivated via a culture of high trust and being able to explore, it is helpful to think of three related elements which deepen our understanding of what makes effective achievement and therefore related feedback: the skill, the will and the thrill (Hattie & Donoghue, 2016).

The skill

We need to know what the students bring to the classroom (re. their skills, will and thrill) and build on this – teaching students the skills to own their own learning; developing multiple learning strategies and knowing when best to apply them; knowing how to focus and narrow the range of reasonable hypotheses to iterate towards to the success criteria; increasing their effort, particularly when the effort leads to tackling more challenging tasks rather than just 'doing more'; and developing effective error detection skills, which lead to students' own self-feedback.

The will

The will relates to the various learning dispositions the student holds. These are discussed in the following section, but the key factor is that learning dispositions are most effective when contextualized rather than dealt with in isolation from the task.

The thrill

We need to help students to be motivated to achieve the success criteria; enhancing the commitment to these criteria; co-constructing success criteria with students and ensuring that they are appropriately specific, clear and challenging - actively involving students in their own learning and training them to be involved in their own self-assessment.

c) Mindsets and mindframes (to be learning ready)

The fixed and growth mindsets

Carol Dweck's fixed and growth mindset research is well-known amongst educators, itself the culmination of 30 odd years of research about motivation. Dweck's work (2000, 2006) led her to believe that there were two core mindsets, or beliefs, that people have about themselves which shape how we approach challenges:

a fixed mindset: the belief that one's abilities cannot be changed, and
a growth mindset: the belief that one's intelligence, skills and qualities can be developed through effort, input and a range of learning strategies.

It is important to determine how and when a growth mindset can be most effective. When students are in situations of not knowing, needing to invest more into learning, and when they make mistakes, then thinking with a growth mindset is particularly enabling (see Hattie, 2017). Thinking with a fixed mindset leads to blaming others, saying you can't do it and resisting or being distracted from learning. We want students to say, 'This is challenging – I can get smarter by doing this' not 'This is challenging – I can't do it'.

Dweck says that saying one has a growth mindset is evidence of a fixed mindset. A growth mindset is instead a way of thinking in a given circumstance, rather than a permanent attribution. We all have moments of fixed and growth mindsets, depending on the circumstances and sometimes a fixed mindset protects us: if I were being confronted by a lion, for instance, it would be appropriate to have a fixed mindset: to give up and hide, rather than believe I can win!

A growth mindset culture, relating to feedback, therefore, is one where students want to challenge themselves, are not afraid of failure or mistakes and know that they can 'grow' their learning. They also know that learning is hard work, have learnt when and how to persist, to seek help and to invest in overlearning so that they can move to more challenging tasks. Teachers who have successfully cultivated student growth mindsets do the following: they model a growth mindset, particularly when students are unsure, making mistakes or engaged in challenging tasks; see mistakes as exciting and precursors of new learning, and they talk about the necessity of struggle in learning and finding oneself in the 'learning pit' (Nottingham, 2017). They live and breathe the appropriate growth language and avoid external rewards, thereby maximizing student self-efficacy. Most importantly, they create high trust for all of this to occur and teach their students how to receive and use the feedback they are given.

Brain development

Research about the brain has shown it has remarkable capacity to grow. Woollett and Maguire (2012), for instance, discovered that 'The Knowledge' learnt by London taxi drivers: the memorization of every street, landmark and building in inner and outer London, had resulted in all drivers monitored having a slightly larger hippocampus (one area of the brain where memory is stored). Neural connections and synapses firing is a subject of great fascination for students of all ages, and a natural starting point in encouraging students to see the potential of their own brains.

We know that the brain goes through much transformation between birth and age 20 (Bolton & Hattie, 2017). We need to know more about these changes in how students process information. As stated by Shayer (2003):

> If you cannot assess the range of mental levels of the children in your class, and simultaneously what is the level of cognitive demand of each of the lesson activities, how can you plan then execute – in response to the minute by minute response of the students – tactics with results in all engaging fruitfully?
>
> *(Shayer, 2003)*

Seeking challenge – using the zones

One of the most effective resources in classrooms to reinforce the 'Goldilocks' principle of aiming for challenge – not too hard, not too easy – is the zoned bullseye diagram as seen in Figure 2.1. By encouraging students to aim for the learning zone (appropriately challenging), rather than the panic zone (too challenging) or the comfort zone (too easy), they are being given permission to seek challenging tasks. For many years, we said the Goldilocks principle was 'not too hard, not too easy' but recent research (Lomas et al., 2017) has shown us it should also be 'not too hard, not too boring'. Students will often willingly undertake very challenging tasks if they find them engaging, want to strive to succeed, have a good sense of what it means to be successful and know a set of strategies for when they get stuck. Never aim for comfort or develop success criteria which are too distant or general as to invoke panic, but make the goal not too hard, not too boring.

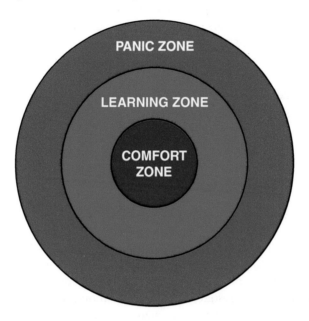

Figure 2.1 The three zones

Although you will see many times throughout this book the aspiration to keep students in the learning or challenge zone, there are exceptions to this! Closed skills with compulsory elements which need to be overlearned in order for them to be stored in our long-term memories (learning tables, how to use speech marks, how to do quadratic equations) always start off in the challenge zone, but necessarily, if learning has happened, move on to the comfort zone. We need to overlearn many of these skills until they become automatic, compressed in our long-term memories, so that we have working memory available to use these skills in new challenging zones.

Manor Primary School in East Sussex extended the zones diagram by giving students colored cards to match the zones, plus a question mark card. Students were encouraged to place the colored card in front of them to match their current thinking and to place the question mark card whenever they needed some coaching from another student. This became a signal to nearby students to spend a few minutes coaching a child who was stuck. A similar technique is the use of colored stacking cups or, as a class, holding up numbers of fingers for answers or whiteboards. Comments from students about the bullseye diagram:

> I like being at green because I want to learn more. I want to learn about making mistakes. I don't want to get it right all the time. I learn more when I make mistakes and fix them.
>
> *Alice, Year 2 (7-year-old)*

> I find my peers will help me when my question mark card is out. They offer to help which means we work it out together and then carry on without an adult.
>
> *George, Year 6 (11-year-old)*

Laura Norcott, a teacher of 5- and 6-year-olds in Harwood Hill School Welwyn Garden City tells her story of the impact of introducing the zones into her classroom:

Before introducing my class to learning zones, I became aware of a high achiever in my class who was unwilling to challenge herself. Over a week I observed how many times she stayed in her comfort zone. On 4 out of 5 mathematics lessons, she went for work that was far too easy and was happy to stay there. If I asked her to try something else, she was unwilling and unmotivated. I spoke with her and she said she was afraid to get things wrong.

Following our discussion on learning zones, I observed her again over a week. This time she chose appropriately challenging activities in all mathematics lessons and was able to use vocabulary associated with the learning zones. She also told me she liked learning from her mistakes.

To further explain the learning zones to the class, I showed the students a video explaining how the brain works and grows when we make mistakes. This engaged the children and made them eager to work outside of their comfort zone.

Quotes from my class:

> **I feel better now that I know it's ok to feel wobbly in the learning zone.**
>
> **If I'm in my panic zone it just means I'm not ready for this yet. I will be one day though!**
>
> **If I'm in my learning zone, it means my brain is working and growing. My brain won't grow if I stay in my comfort zone.**
>
> *(Laura Norcott)*

I conducted a survey by asking the students to answer some key questions, both before and after the introduction of the learning zones:

	Before introducing learning zones	After working with learning zones for 2 weeks
I always choose something easy	27%	16%
I ask for help straight away	23%	9%
I enjoy my work more when it is easy	43%	16%
I like it when my work is easy because I get more work done	63%	19%
I am not learning anything if my work is too easy	20%	41%

Deliberate practice, spaced not massed

We know that to develop skills we all need multiple practice opportunities, underpinned by specific, clear goal-based instruction. The term 'deliberate practice' (Ericsson, Krampe & Tesch-Romer, 1993) refers to practice which is not just repeated exercises of the same thing, but works hand in hand with specific skill building, deliberate teaching, feedback and success criteria – always pushing the boundaries, so that the 'just right' zone increases in its demands as the students gain competence.

The message here is that practice alone might not be enough – it needs to be practice alongside improvement, hence the term 'deliberate practice'. We need help from teachers and peers to improve as we practice; to continually alter, adjust and learn from previous attempts and trials; to increase the degree of challenge with the intention of mastering the skill we are practicing. This is where openness to feedback and making errors as we reach the edge of our skills combine with effective teaching to maximize learning capacity.

An overloaded curriculum tends to encourage teachers to overemphasize content and divide learning into segments which are taught in one go and seldom revisited, except for test purposes. Contrary to this model, deeper learning occurs when curriculum items or generic skills are frequently revisited or 'spaced' rather than 'massed' – that is learnt over time not all at once (d = 0.60). Nuthall (2005), as stated earlier, found that all students, high or low achievers, often needed three to five exposures to the learning – usually over several days – before there was a reasonable probability that they would learn.

Sometimes our success is measured when we do not know we know: that is, when our learning has become automatic. When that happens, we have so over-learned something, we can immediately recall and use that knowledge in new situations. When we were learning to walk there were many bumps, trials, errors and hurts, but, once mastered, we do not consciously think about moving one foot in front of the other – we have overlearned how to walk. The same is true of times tables, spellings, writing sentences and so on. After being exposed to the principles of why $6 \times 9 = 54$, there comes a time when it is powerful to overlearn this, so that it can be immediately retrieved and used for problem solving, making deeper relations, and in further mathematics. We are of little brains – most of us can process about 4 to 6 things in our working memory, so those students who must work out 6×9 are using their working memory space for this are disadvantaged, while those who automatically know that $6 \times 9 = 54$ can use their working memory to use this knowledge to do other things.

The language of learning

> When tasks are more complex for a student, the quality of meta-cognitive skills rather than intellectual ability is the main determinant of learning outcomes.
>
> *(Hattie, 2009)*

Learning dispositions

The terms learning 'powers' are often used to describe the learning dispositions identified by researchers such as Guy Claxton (2002) and Art Costa and Kallick (2008). Meta-cognitive strategies, or thinking about thinking, have an effect size of 0.69. The three major elements of meta-cognition are:

- disinhibition – or the skill of not being distracted or stuck on one phase,
- updating and monitoring of what we are learning, and,
- the skill of shifting between tasks, or ways of attacking problems.

These three together form what is called executive functioning, meta cognition or self-regulation. Various researchers have defined learning as a number of dispositions, including Claxton's '4 Rs': resilience, reciprocity, resourcefulness and reflectiveness (2002) and Costa and Kallick's 'Habits of Mind' (2008). These 'habits of mind' relate to knowing how to behave intelligently when you do not know the answer or are 'stuck', and include persisting, managing impulsivity, listening with understanding and empathy, thinking flexibly, taking responsible risks, striving for accuracy, questioning and posing problems, applying past knowledge to new situations and remaining open to continuous learning. All are part of meta-cognition – our knowledge of how we think and learn.

These are dispositions which give us the language of learning but need to be integrated into lessons and included within the various contexts of learning to be effective.

An example of their use

A synthesis of Claxton and Costa's dispositions was given to teachers over several years in evaluation teams of teachers (Clarke, 2014):

Concentrate (Disinhibit)	Manage distractions Get lost in the task Do one thing at a time Break things down Plan and think it through Draw diagrams, jot down thoughts or things which help you think
Don't give up (Persistence)	Work hard Practice lots Keep going Try new strategies Ask for help Start again Take a brain break
Be cooperative (Work with others)	Listen to others Say when you don't understand Be kind when you disagree Explain things to help others Be tolerant
Be curious (Shift between ideas)	Ask questions Notice things Look for patterns and connections Think of possible reasons Research Ask 'What if . . .?'
Have a go (Learn from errors)	Think with a growth mindset Don't worry if it goes wrong Learn from mistakes Be excited to try new things
Use your imagination (Think outside the box)	Be creative Let your imagination go Think up new ideas and questions
Keep improving (Learn to learn)	Keep reviewing your work Identify your best bits Improve one thing first Try to be better than last time Don't compare yourself to others, only yourself! Take small steps
Enjoy learning (Experience the joy of learning)	Feel proud of all your achievements Feel your neurons connecting! Imagine your intelligence growing by the minute! Use what you have learnt in real life Know you can do it if you have input and you practice

Teachers used these 'learning powers' in different ways, but always aiming for a 'split screen' approach (Claxton, 2002), where the focused learning power has *equal status* to the knowledge or skill learning intention of the lesson. One of the more successful strategies has been to attach a 'character' to each of the eight categories, write a story for the character in which the various elements are explored then use this story to introduce the particular learning power to the class (see below for an example of a story and character for early years by Charlotte Rollinson from Thameside School, Reading). Teachers usually focus on one story a week, displaying the characters and their breakdown of skills, until all the categories are known.

Concentrate: Kuba caterpillar

Once upon a time there was a family of caterpillars – Mummy caterpillar, Daddy caterpillar and their son, Kuba the caterpillar. One day, Mummy caterpillar asked Kuba to go out and collect some leaves for dinner. As he set off he met his friend Tom, who wanted to go and play football. But Kuba said 'No, I need to collect my leaves'. A bit later, he met his cousin Kasper, who asked him to go to his house for lemonade, but again, Kuba said 'No, I have to collect leaves. I need to concentrate on what Mummy asked me to do'. When he had finished collecting leaves, he went home and told his Mummy what his friends had said. 'Well done Kuba for concentrating on what I asked you to do, now you have finished, you can go and play!'

Charlotte explains:

Children had opportunities to learn about these animals through the week and colour in/draw their own pictures of the characters. We would discuss with the children different ways they could use the character to help them in school, for example how they could 'have a go' around the classroom. The children would then be praised for the focus aspect of the week all week by all adults in the classroom and encouraged to use the words with each other. Once the children had learnt all 8 elements of being a successful learner, for each lesson taking place, the adults and children would choose the characters they would particularly need to use in that lesson to help them learn. These characters would then be stuck to the board underneath the learning intention and success criteria to remind the children.

The children have really taken to these characters, with the children being very concerned when I borrowed 2 for a day! Comments from Foundation Stage, Kindergarten students include:

- Kuba helps us to learn nicely (Joshua, age 4).
- When Kuba's friends say does he want to play he says no because he's busy. He's concentrating (Eva, age 5).

- The caterpillar works hard. He's ignoring the children playing (Henry, age 4).

(Charlotte Rollinson, Thameside School)

Students from Rockcastle County High School, Mount Vernon, Kentucky, given the same learning 'powers', chose Disney characters to represent each element. Their knowledge of each character's attitude and personality helped them connect with the dispositions. It appears that creating links with characters, real or imagined, who embody the appropriate characteristics of the learning dispositions, works for students of all ages.

(Examples taken from Outstanding Formative Assessment, Clarke, 2014)

Lists of learning dispositions can be easily disregarded by students and teachers if not embedded in contexts and lessons. Equal status, of course, means that they have to be referred to as much as the skill intentions. So, feedback would include information about those elements as well as the skill level (e.g. *You worked very well cooperating with your learning partner to improve both pieces of work / You were managing distractions and concentrating during that challenge*).

The ten mindframes for teachers and students

The ten mindframes, derived from 'Visible Learning' research, add yet more dimensions to the concept of an evaluative mindset and learning dispositions (Hattie & Zierer, 2018). The mindframes for teachers and how they relate to those of their students:

Teacher	⟶	Student
I am an evaluator of my impact on student learning.	Are our practices bringing out the best in our students?	I am an evaluator of my learning.
I see assessment as feedback to me.	Are we using assessment information to progress student achievement and to help us plan next teaching steps?	I give feedback to my teachers and receive it from them and my peers to help my learning progress.
I collaborate with others about my concepts of progress and impact.	Are we isolated teachers, or do we work with other teachers and our students about what we mean by progress and impact?	I collaborate with my peers about what I mean by progress and success in learning. I am an assessment capable learner.

(continued overleaf)

I am a change agent and believe all students can learn.	Are school leaders establishing a climate that creates a high sense of teacher self-efficacy, so that teachers can work together as change agents, knowing they are truly significant in every student's life?	I have a high sense of self-efficacy.
I strive for challenge.	Do we encourage a mindset in which mistakes are an essential feature in learning? Do teachers and students strive to be in the learning zone rather than the comfort zone?	I enjoy and seek challenging tasks.
I give and help students understand feedback and I interpret and act on feedback to me.	I not only give feedback to students, I help them understand and act on this feedback, and I continually seek feedback from my students to help me plan future teaching.	I know how to give, receive and use feedback about my learning.
I talk about learning and not about teaching.	Are we discussing the learning more than the teaching or vice versa?	I talk about what I am learning not what I am doing.
I engage in as much dialogue as monologue.	Do we listen to students or do we continue with what we want to say? Can I create discussions with and among my students?	I value the different social and cognitive pairings in lessons and learn from the dialogue I have with my peers.
I explicitly inform students what successful impact looks like from the outset.	I show students near the start of lessons what success looks like. I often work with them to understand what this success means and provide feedback of how they are moving towards it.	I use personal bests to understand how far I am from meeting the success criteria of the lesson.
I build relationships and trust so that learning can occur in a place where it is safe to make mistakes and learn from others.	I build safe and fair environments so that students can make errors, learn from theirs and others' mistakes, and move into the challenge zone of learning.	I feel valued, respected, liked and listened to by my teachers. I offer them the same courtesy.
I focus on learning and the language of learning.	Are we discussing the learning more than the teaching or vice versa? Do we have common language about learning via learning dispositions, learning intentions and success criteria?	I talk about what I am learning, not what I am doing.

Various types of feedback are outlined in this book, alongside the relevant research evidence, but, as with any strategy, it is how it's done that makes the difference between success and failure. The ten mindframes go a long way to ensuring a foundation of appropriate mindsets, beliefs and practices so that feedback strategies can be authentically and effectively put into practice.

The core notion here is that students need teaching to develop multiple strategies and executive control, and thence feedback about the strategies can be as critical as feedback about the content which the strategies are addressing. Knowing the strategies, knowing when to apply them, knowing to be flexible if the strategy is not working all require feedback from the teacher; feedback which the teacher also requires when their strategies are not having the desired impact on student learning.

Integrating mindsets and mindframes – practical examples

The 'Learning and Teaching Group' led by Midlothian Education Services in Scotland developed the following graphic (Figure 2.2) with the aim of bringing together the characteristics of assessment capable (visible) learners, growth mindset, challenge and learning dispositions into an aspiration for all Midlothian learners. The intention was that this would apply for lifelong learning, not just the school years.

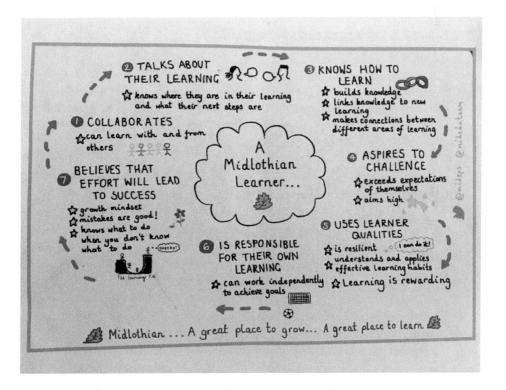

Figure 2.2 A Midlothian learner

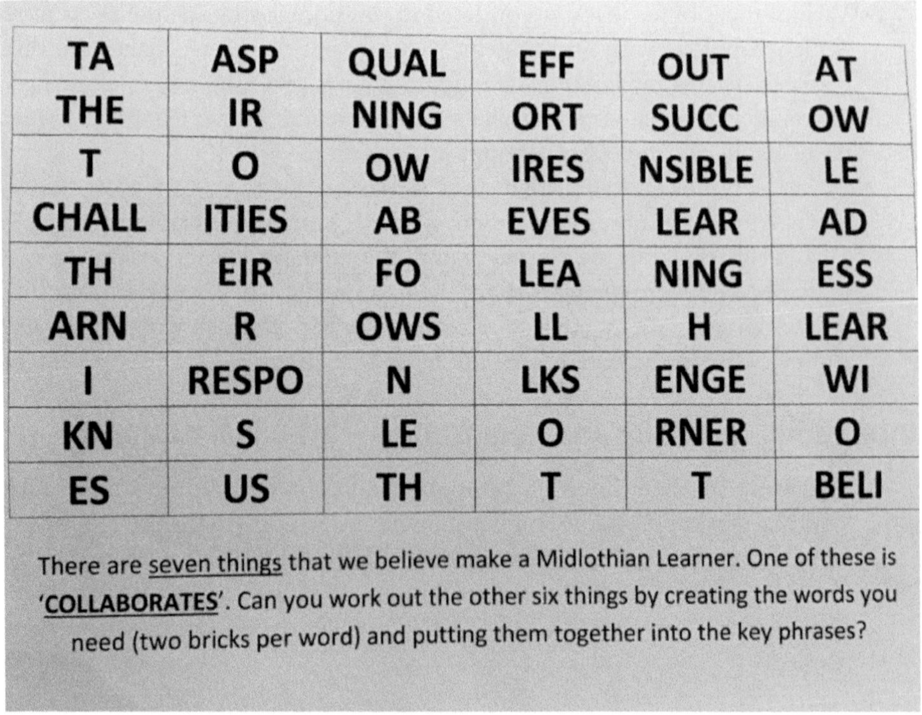

TA	ASP	QUAL	EFF	OUT	AT
THE	IR	NING	ORT	SUCC	OW
T	O	OW	IRES	NSIBLE	LE
CHALL	ITIES	AB	EVES	LEAR	AD
TH	EIR	FO	LEA	NING	ESS
ARN	R	OWS	LL	H	LEAR
I	RESPO	N	LKS	ENGE	WI
KN	S	LE	O	RNER	O
ES	US	TH	T	T	BELI

There are <u>seven things</u> that we believe make a Midlothian Learner. One of these is '**COLLABORATES**'. Can you work out the other six things by creating the words you need (two bricks per word) and putting them together into the key phrases?

Figure 2.3 Involving students in the graphic

Teachers were given suggestions of how the graphic could be introduced to students so that it did not become 'wallpaper'. Colin Burt, a teacher at Roslin School, described how he went about involving older students in the concepts:

As a class we spoke about what could make a 'Midlothian learner'. The class came up with a number of words which were not recorded so that the discussion would flow. I then introduced the class to the brick wall (Figure 2.3) and asked if they could work out the phrases. They were given a large sheet of paper, with the preprinted word 'collaborates' in the center, to glue the phrases on. After the phrases had been correctly found the class tried to match the phrases to their meanings.

Another school, Hawthornden, modified the graphic as follows (Figure 2.4), bringing in more 'Visible Learning' links:

Teachers at Hawthornden said that they first focused on 'talking about our learning' and reflected that students were aware that this means talking about themselves as a learner in terms of their learning goals and their next steps. The students now identify that 'talking about our learning' happens during peer and

COLLABORATES	• Exceeds expectations of themselves • Aims high
TALKS ABOUT THEIR LEARNING	• Builds knowledge • Links knowledge to new learning • Makes connections between different areas of learning
KNOWS HOW TO LEARN	• Is resilient • (I can do it!) • Understands and applies effective learning habits • Learning is rewarding
ASPIRES TO CHALLENGE	• Can work independently to achieve goals
USES LEARNER QUALITIES	• Knows where they are in their learning and what their next steps are
IS RESPONSIBLE FOR THEIR OWN LEARNING	• Growth mindset • Mistakes are good! • Knows what to do when you don't know what to do (the Learning Pit!)
BELIEVES THAT EFFORT WILL LEAD TO SUCCESS	• Can learn with and from others

Figure 2.4 'A Midlothian learner' in graphic form – matching to ensure engagement and understanding task

self-assessment, by discussing learning intentions and success criteria and reflecting in their reflection jotters or learning logs.

As a school, it was decided to augment the current practice by having more open afternoons built into the school calendar for PATPAL (pupils as teachers/parents as learners in which students taught their parents something they were learning in their classroom); establishing frequent opportunities for students to share and talk about their learning such as weekly plans, citizenship lessons and assemblies; feedback to incorporate all areas of the curriculum and changing the ethos of sharing summative evaluation with students openly rather than not allowing them to see them.

The Midlothian graphic forms not only the basis of teaching and learning but also gives all involved appropriate language to describe their learning. The words we use convey and form our attitudes, so if students start using these words and phrases in their conversations to each other about their learning, not only are they influencing their thoughts and actions, but they form evidence of their internalization of the concepts. Whichever strategy schools use to introduce and embed learning dispositions, what matters is that they are used and discussed and linked hand in hand with learning intentions and success criteria rather than as supplementary optional ideas.

The following graphic from The Australian International School in Malaysia (Figure 2.5) expresses similar values and aims:

Figure 2.5 An inspired and passionate teacher

(Credits: Australian International School Malaysia)

d) Normalizing and celebrating error

A key component of effective feedback is the universal attitude in a school community towards error: being stuck, making mistakes, having a misconception. Historically these have been associated with 'being wrong', something to be ashamed of, to cover up or erase, for fear of perceptions of failure to have met teacher or parental expectations. An all too typical reaction by teachers is to not dwell on error for fear of affecting a student's self-esteem – especially in front of their peers. A key study (Moser et al., 2011) confirmed that when we make errors there are increased signals to our brain processing to reflect our heightened attention to these mistakes. When we make a mistake, the brain has two potential responses: 1) an 'ERN (feedback error-related negativity) response' which is an increase of electrical activity when the brain experiences conflict between a correct response and an error and 2) 'a Pe (error positivity) response' which is a brain signal thought to reflect conscious attention to mistakes. Put simply, mistakes can lead to what Piaget called disequilibrium – an upset between what we know and do not know – and this can be a critical moment for learning to occur. We must seize the moment to ensure we deal with these tensions, as the understanding. Even with no correction of the error, because it is a time of struggle, there is brain activity because we are being challenged and therefore ripe for learning.

As stated in 'Visible Learning for Teachers':

> Feedback is most effective when students do not have proficiency or mastery – and thus it thrives when there is error or incomplete knowing and understanding. Errors invite opportunity. They should not be seen as embarrassments, signs of failure or something to be avoided. They are exciting, because they indicate a tension between what we now know and what we could know: they are signs of opportunities to learn and they are to be embraced.
>
> *(Hattie, 2012)*

Feedback is most powerful when it addresses faulty interpretations and not lack of understanding. Clearly feedback is part of the learning process, coming after initial instruction, with information provided regarding some aspect of the students' performance. When the initial teaching, however, is seen by the student as unfamiliar or difficult to understand, feedback is of little use, hence the vital importance of student voice in articulating lack of understanding:

> If the material studied is unfamiliar or abstruse, providing feedback should have little effect on criterion performance, since there is no way to relate the new information to what is already known.
>
> *(Kulhavy, 1977)*

Errors in learning can create opportunities, can lead to feedback, can help realize connections, can be a by-product of active learning and can be most positive. Errors can be upsetting, disruptive and frustrating and can lower motivation to engage, learn and continue, precisely why the culture of normalizing and celebrating error is so important.

Errors can include:

- Applying the most accessible strategy even if it's the wrong one
- Using old routines and discounting unique aspects of the current problem

- Ignoring critical information and knowledge
- Over reliance of easily obtained information
- Giving greater weight to objective or surface information over deeper understanding
- Over focus on simple connections or solutions when more complicated solutions are needed
- Too readily discounting competing explanations
- Working backwards in the wrong way from a pre-ordained solution
- Not exploring errors in an earlier analysis
- Rejecting risk and therefore making mistakes when taking a risk would result in correct answers or higher achievement
- Over optimism about a suggested solution – accepting strategies without analyzing whether they will be the right one
- Failure to commit so unfocused
- Underestimating time and resources needed for the solution
- Working automatically instead of thinking more creatively and exploring different strategies

There are so many ways to productively fail! However, as Michael Jordan famously said:

> I've missed more than 9000 shots in my career. I've lost almost 300 games. Twenty-six times I've been trusted to take the game winning shot and missed. I've failed over and over and over again in my life. And that is why I succeed.

Much of a teacher's time is spent spotting misconceptions and slips (errors which are the result of inattention rather than misconception). If students are on the wrong track and have no way of finding out for themselves, then a key characteristic of the teacher's job is to find the best way of dealing with misconceptions and other errors. Misconceptions usually need more input, from the most skilled explainer, whereas slips are easier to deal with: they can usually be sorted out by the student if time is given for them to reread their work, read it out loud or check their calculations.

One strategy for getting students to rethink their mistakes first is to ask them to circle where they think they might have gone wrong (Didau, 2015). Another strategy for encouraging another look at the work, but also to give the message that mistakes are a vital part of learning, is to draw a heart around the mistake. This can be done by the teacher on the move around the classroom as well as during after lesson marking, if that is deemed to be appropriate for this particular focus. Self-marking given a set of answers also encourages students to unpick their calculations or written accounts and make corrections unaided or know where to seek further feedback.

Other strategies include: creating a risk-free zone in lessons where students can provide conjectures and ideas rather than fully formed thoughts or feeling they can only speak when they know the right answer; sending them (at the right time) into the learning pit (see Nottingham 2017); handing the errors back to the student to work through with you and the class and asking for more appropriate alternative strategies to show the value of making mistakes.

Key points

- *When students are learning content and the surface aspects of learning it is probably better to provide corrective feedback and move on.*
- *When students have acquired surface knowledge, however, and are starting to see connections and think more deeply, this is where errors and the subsequent discussion and analysis of these are most powerful.*

Teachers' responses to error

There are major differences between cultures in how error is dealt with by teachers. US and Chinese students make the same amount of errors, but US teachers tend to immediately correct them whereas Chinese teachers ask follow-up questions to promote student discussion (Tulis, 2013). Western countries tend to want to protect self-esteem, reduce any negative affect and privately correct errors. Indeed, Tulis (2013) showed that when a student makes an error in front of their peers, 40–50% of the time teachers correct the error, 40–50% of the time teachers ask another student to correct the error, 5–10% of the time they ignore the error and only 5–10% of the time do they use the error to advance learning. Other countries, where schooling is less focused on developing socialization, are more likely to encourage and use errors, publicly address errors and share wrong solutions as learning opportunities (Boaler, 2016).

A study by Steuer, Rosentritt-Brunn and Dresel (2013) which looked at the impact of 'mistakes friendly' classrooms, and 'mistakes unfriendly' classrooms found that when students perceived their classroom as mistakes friendly – above and beyond other aspects of their classroom environment – they increased their effort in their learning.

The normalizing and celebrating of mistakes has clear implications for the ways in which teachers respond to error. There should be no occurrence when responses lead to shame and disapproval, but instead feedback linking error to 'where to next' information can be most worthwhile – the link to new learning. When students make errors, these should be highlighted in a positive way, used as opportunities to relearn, shared as learning opportunities for others and seen as the road to mastery. Teachers who provide opportunities to discuss student misconceptions and errors and encourage students to learn from errors by self-correcting, foster more confidence in trying a range of strategies to deal with mistakes (Tulis, 2013). It matters that they do this in a climate of high trust not only between the teacher and student, but also among the students, where all are safe from ridicule. A safe environment is needed to see errors as powerful.

Celebrating and dealing with error – practical strategies

We noted above that using growth mindset thinking has powerful effects in situations where errors abound. Dweck gave helpful advice about what to say and what not to say when children experience difficulty, especially in mathematics. Sympathy is avoided – instead error receives excitement about the learning to follow. Notice the lack of superlatives or personal ego-related remarks:

Growth mindset (What to say)	Fixed mindset (What not to say)
'When you learn how to do a new kind of problem, it grows your math learning!'	'Not everybody is good at math. Just do your best'.
'If you catch yourself saying, 'I'm not a math person,' just add the word 'yet' to the end of the sentence'.	'That's ok, maybe math is not one of your strengths'.
'That feeling of math being hard is the feeling of your math knowledge growing'.	'Don't worry, you'll get it if you keep trying'. *If students are using the wrong strategies, their efforts might not work. Plus, they may feel particularly inept if their efforts are fruitless.*
'The point isn't to get it all right away. The point is to grow your understanding step by step. What can you try next?'	'Great effort! You tried your best'.

(Dweck, 2015)

One lesson observed, in a class of 9-year-olds in St. Luke's School in Westminster, cultivated and celebrated error throughout, with an insistence that new learning should take place:

Learning intention: estimating weight, knowing how many grams in a kilogram

The teacher, Seamus Gibbons, had prepared trays of school weights wrapped in tissue paper, ranging from 1 gram to 1 kilogram. The students were asked to put them in order of weight and to attach sticky notes to each estimating what they weighed. Various outrageous weights were written, such as 34 tons, 25 kilograms, even zero. Then came the reveal, in which the students tore off the wrapping and saw what their weights really weighed. There were shrieks of laughter as they saw how far out their estimates were.

A critical teaching point occurred at this moment. Seamus showed a picture of a polar bear and told them a polar bear weighs approximately one ton, then a picture of an elephant which they were told weighed between 7 and 10 tons. A bag of sugar and a credit card followed.

To celebrate their mistakes, the students were then given exit slips as follows:

My wonderful mistake	What I learnt

As each child came to the door with their completed slip, Seamus read it then commented, sending the child back to be more accurate or write more detail if he felt they had rushed this. After several minutes, only two children remained who he asked to get the one-gram weight and talk about how many grams in a kilogram. Apart from the clear message that learning follows mistakes, the last few minutes were particularly striking: the capitalizing on the moment, ensuring that every child had some understanding of how many grams made a kilogram. Had he simply taken the exit slips and looked at them away from the children, those golden moments when the lesson content was still active would be gone, and those children who needed more 1–1 coaching would probably never have been given the chance, in context, to consolidate their learning. Capitalizing on the moment, a key feature of effective feedback, is revisited throughout this book.

(Video of this lesson is available from www.shirleyclarke-education.org)

A major benefit of students having co-constructed success criteria is that they have a reference to understand more clearly when they have made an error or have not fulfilled expectations of the task. The same is true when lessons have included analysis of examples of excellence, and students have been given scoring rubrics well before they complete the work (and well before the work is assessed).

Asking students to identify mistakes projected via an example of work from a student from a previous year or class is a powerful way of determining what students already know as well as demonstrating that error invites feedback and therefore new learning. 'Where is the error in this calculation?' is an effective starting point to a lesson, as it reveals prior knowledge, encourages cooperative analysis and discussion, focuses on success criteria and possibly shows what excellence looks like, all setting the scene for targeted and focused feedback.

An example of spotting errors for 6- and 7-year-olds

Which is 31? A or B? Convince your talk/learning partner . . .

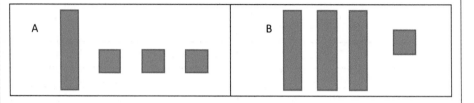

An example of spotting errors for 13-year-olds

What went wrong here? Discuss . . .

How many sweets altogether? 26, 26, 26, 26, 26, 26, 26

×	20	7
6	120	42

Answer: 26 × 7 = 162

Spoiler: the student has created a multiplication grid for 27 × 6 rather than 26 × 7.

By featuring mistakes in this way, error is normalized and used to further learning. Asking students to share their 'marvelous mistake' in a classroom where challenge is the norm has many benefits. By going through the error, which other students will also probably have made, the value of mistakes is exemplified, and its analysis helps all students learn more deeply.

James Gleeson, a teacher from Brisbane Grammar School, has identified six types of error common in students' mathematics (Figures 2.6–2.9)

Error types – explanatory notes

Figure 2.6 can be used to place student errors into categories. This may reveal patterns in the types of errors most commonly made. Students are asked to review their examination script and identify questions in which they did not receive full marks. With the guidance of their teacher, students are encouraged to look more closely at the mistakes they have made and create an error matrix that quantifies the number of errors that fall into each category.

During the reflection component of the task, students are asked to use the results of their personal error analysis to identify areas of strength and areas in which they would like to improve. With further guidance and support from their teacher, students set goals for their next unit of work, based on what they have discovered about their own learning.

Reading (R)	The student has misread the question. For example, a question on calculating the area of a shape follows a perimeter question and the student has not read carefully enough to notice the change in the instructions. He calculates the perimeter rather than the area. Another example is misreading 'What fraction of the marbles are not red?' as 'What fraction of the marbles are red?' and thereby not answering the question that has been asked.
Acquisition of knowledge (A)	The student does not appear to have acquired the knowledge needed to access the question and make meaningful progress towards the answer. This may be the result of not acquiring knowledge of the meaning of mathematical terms, for example 'scalene' or 'factorize', but also the non-acquisition of relevant concepts or procedures, which may require further dedicated investigation.
Strategic (S)	*Applies only to questions that require students to determine for themselves which knowledge and procedures are required, or that require the application of Mathematical knowledge in new or unfamiliar contexts.* The student has demonstrated reliable knowledge of the relevant concepts, ideas and procedures in his lessons or in other assessed responses, but after reading this unfamiliar question he was not able to identify that these were the ideas or procedures that were needed. He was not able to organize his acquired knowledge into a cohesive strategy to solve the problem.
Execution of knowledge (E)	The student has made a mistake in one or more steps of a well-established or internalized routine or procedure. There should be evidence in his recent class work or in other assessed responses that he can reliably reproduce the procedure with accuracy, for example as revealed in the preceding or succeeding questions, but he has not replicated the procedure accurately in this case. Sometimes these errors result from a need to work more carefully and methodically or with better 'setting out', such as when not lining up place value columns or when misreading previously written digits due to poor handwriting or rushed work.
Calculations (C)	In earlier years this refers to the student making a mistake when mentally calculating a simple addition, subtraction, multiplication or division. For example, a times table or simple mental addition. In later years this can expanded to include errors associated with entering incorrect digits into the calculator or some other error arising from an operation performed on the calculator.
Findings (F)	The student has completed the question correctly and found the correct answer, but they have not presented their answer using established conventions or have not interpreted their findings in the context of the question. For example, not presenting units for measurements, not constructing a final sentence to communicate the answer to a word-based problem or stating an answer such as '2.63 busses are needed to transport the children'.

Figure 2.6 Six common errors

James converted these to more student friendly language (Figure 2.7).

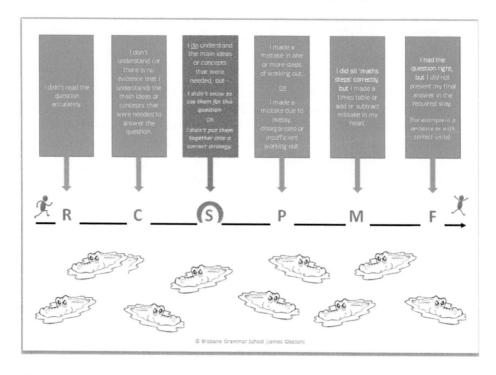

Figure 2.7 Student friendly errors

So far, the types of error have been identified, but these are only useful if both teachers and students know what to do to help them learn from these errors. The following student guide provides exactly that (Figure 2.8).

Finally, Figure 2.9 gives students aged 13–15 helpful tips for avoiding over-whelming working memory when learning mathematical procedures and concepts.

How can I learn from my mistakes in mathematics?

I am making Reading (R) mistakes. I can…

- Slow down a little and read questions more carefully.
- Read questions twice before starting.
- Use a highlighter or underline key words, clue words or instructions.
- Use a checking technique – look at my final answer, then reread the question once more before starting the next question.
- Before handing in my work, check through it for reading mistakes.

I am making Acquisition of Knowledge (A) mistakes. I can…

- Watch the videos on My Grammar a number of times. Take notes about important examples or information in the videos. Ask a parent, sibling or my teacher if I do not understand what has been explained in the videos.
- Go to Pythagoras Club for some extra help with my maths.
- See my teacher before school to get help when I don't understand something. Ask them to explain it to me in a different way.
- Ask a parent or older brother or sister to help me when I don't understand my homework.
- Research other explanations of concepts when I don't understand (e.g. Look up the work on the Hot Maths website).

I am making Strategic (S) mistakes. I can…

- Practice more worded questions and problem-solving questions in my text book and on My Grammar.
- Practice level three and challenge level questions on Hot Maths more often.
- Show my teacher my practice of problem solving or worded questions if I am getting them wrong.
- Spend more time learning the key terms, definitions, clue words or phrases. Use flash cards or memory cards to help me consolidate and maintain my knowledge of these.
- Focus on understanding the main ideas, techniques and procedures at a deeper level rather than just learning 'how to do it'.
- Listen more carefully to class discussions about harder questions and make a time with my teacher if I do not understand the examples of harder work covered in class.

Figure 2.8 Learning from mistakes student guide (*continued overleaf*)

I am making Execution of Knowledge (E) mistakes. I can...

- Do more detailed, neat and accurate working out.
- Set my work out more clearly so I don't get confused.
- Line up my columns more accurately so that I don't get mixed up with where digits are supposed to be.
- Use estimation or checking techniques to confirm that my answer is reasonable.
- Don't rush. Give the execution of each technique or procedure my full attention before moving the focus of my concentration to other things.
- Write a list of steps for the main procedures during my study.
- Make sure I <u>understand</u> what each step in a procedure does and how each step gets me closer to the answer. Ask my teacher if I need help with this.
- Focus on proving why my answer is correct, not just writing an answer.
- Provide more working out to support my answer and show why it is correct.

I am making Calculation (C) mistakes. I can...

- Practice times tables, divisions and 2-digit additions and subtractions more regularly.
- Have a parent (or brother or sister) ask me number facts questions at home each day.
- Slow down a little. Avoid rushing and making mistakes.
- Try to focus on each calculation one at a time before moving on to the next.
- Leave time to go back and check for mental calculation errors.
- Do calculations on the calculator twice.
- Slow down when using the calculator.
- Stop and consider if the result of a calculation makes sense before continuing.
- Estimate what the result of a calculation should be before starting.

I am making Findings (F) mistakes. I can...

- Remember that any worded questions need a sentence which states the final answer.
- Remember that questions involving time, money, mass, area etc. must have units (e.g. minutes, $, kg, m^2).
- Before moving on to the next question, re-read the current question to make sure I have interpreted my answer correctly.
- Make sure my answer is in the required format.
- Provide more detail when stating my answer.
- Read my concluding sentence over again to make sure it answers the question and will make sense to the reader.

Figure 2.8 (*Continued*)

Year 8–10 level (Ages 13–15)

Acquiring reliable knowledge of new mathematical procedures

- Create a check list of steps for the procedure and check each step off as I do it during my practice.
- Engage in more distributed practice of key procedures. Keep a record of dates, topics and time spent. Show my teacher my records and the questions I practiced at the end of each week.
- Create a mnemonic, acronym or rhyme to help remember all the steps.
- Create a flow chart that gives a visual representation of the procedure and how it all fits together.
- Create an annotated list of steps. For each step, give an explanation of why this step is needed. Read this regularly and refer to it whenever I practice this procedure.
- Conduct more distributed practice, focusing on doing each step fully and accurately. As I work, stop and check that each step is correct and error free before proceeding to the next step.

Acquiring reliable knowledge of new mathematical concepts

- Approach my teacher and set up a regular time each week during which I will get some help.
- Ask for help from a tutor, parent, sibling, friend or class mate.
- Draw diagrams (such as mind maps or concept maps). These will help me visualize the main ideas, understand how concepts work and build awareness of how concepts fit together to form the 'big picture'.
- Research, read and take notes on 2 alternative explanations for the concept found on reliable internet sites or in available textbooks. Show my completed notes to my teacher.
- Check My Grammar and Shared OneNotes for extra resources (power points, animations, tutorials) that have been provided by other teachers.
- Go to maths sites online (for example you tube, purple maths, BBC bitesize or khan academy) and find lessons, interactive activities or video tutorials on this topic.

Figure 2.9 Learning mathematical procedures and concepts

e) Equity in learning through mixed ability

The culture outlined in this section includes students from across the distribution of achievement working together, as then errors and the place of feedback can be maximized. The overuse of ability grouping, thus, can be a major barrier for students realizing the power of feedback. Placing students in ability groups so often sets false expectations about whether a student is seen by the school as a winner or loser; it can lock step students into the ability group, and often, without exposure to appropriate material, they cannot climb out of a lower group even if they are capable, a late developer, or become more invested in learning. The research on the negative equity effects of ability grouping are damning. If you are in the top or bottom group, then why invest in learning when the system has already made its decision?

Many schools still use some kind of ability grouping, usually for mathematics but sometimes other subjects. This is manifested by labeled groups in class or tracking (known as setting in the UK), despite evidence that ability grouping is detrimental to students' self-efficacy and, because of the labeling, so often becomes a self-fulfilling prophecy. And on top of this there are the major equity issues with minority students in the lower classes and too often the lesser experienced and expert teachers assigned to lower tracks (Chiu, Chow and Joh, 2017).

A recent study by Francis, Archer, Hodgen, Pepper, Taylor and Travers (2016), tried to understand why there is the continuation of ability grouping in England. They found that the problem lay *mainly* with policy makers' edicts to schools and their drive to continually 'raise standards'. In the Government White Paper to schools in 2005, *'Higher standards, better schools for all'*, for instance, it was explained:

> Grouping students can help to build motivation, social skills and independence; and most importantly can raise standards because students are better engaged in their own learning. We have encouraged schools to use setting (tracking) since 1997.
>
> *(DCSF, 2005)*

Clearly such evidence-free edicts do not help.

Five hundred studies from 14 meta-analyses on ability grouping resulted in an effect size of 0.12 – a very low impact on student achievement, with outcomes of very little change in attainment but profound effects on student efficacy (Hattie, 2009).

Stigler and Hiebert (1999), in their inspirational book 'The Teaching Gap', outline the differences between Japanese classes that were high achieving and comparatively lower achieving American classes. One of the key differences was that US teachers see mixed ability as a problem whereas Japanese teachers see mixed ability as a gift. Individual differences are seen as beneficial for the class because they produce a range of ideas, methods and solutions that provide the material for student discussion and reflection. Far eastern countries, which feature at the top of various world league tables (e.g. Pisa) do not use ability groups, seeing differences within class as essential to cooperative learning for all. In Finland, also a leading light in education, ability grouping is illegal before the age of 15.

One of the more famous experiments in education was conducted by Rosenthal and Jacobson (1968), called the Pygmalion effect. Pygmalion was a Greek sculptor who fell in love with a statue of a beautiful woman he carved. He kissed and doted on the statue which then turned into a woman, and his expectations were realized. Similarly, Rosenthal and Jacobson told teachers that half of their students were late bloomers and would 'bloom' during the year and half would not, based on tests that they had administered. This was all fictitious as the 'late bloomers' were chosen randomly. Sure enough, at the end of the year more 'bloomers' outperformed 'non-bloomers'. Given the assignment was random, the difference claimed was a function of the higher expectations of the teachers about these students.

This led to many people hunting for the sources of teachers' higher expectations in any situation. Was it to do with gender, ethnicity, social class, stereotyping, diagnostic labels, physical attractiveness, language style, the age of the student, personality or social skills, the relationship between teacher and student, background, names, other siblings or one-parent families? None of these really succeeded in explaining the source of teacher expectations. Christine Rubie-Davies (2017) argued that this was based on a misunderstanding, as the most important implication was that teachers who had high expectations tended to have them for all the students, and teachers who had low expectations again tended to have them for all the students. She waited a month into the school year until teachers had formed their own views about students, tested the students, gave the teachers the results, and then asked them to predict the students' attainment by the end of the year. Those teachers who had high expectations were more likely to enhance their students' learning, whereas those who had low expectations hardly changed the students' growth over a year.

Mixed ability strategies

Teach students the same syllabus – don't limit expectations

Boaler (2016) describes how most secondary schools in the UK decide, through ability grouping or setting, which students should sit the lower GCSE mathematics exam, with a maximum C grade limit, or the higher paper, with A★ as the maximum grade. One secondary school in England decided to enter all students for the higher GCSE exam, regardless of their previous achievement, and organized the curriculum coverage accordingly. The results were dramatic, with A★ to C rates jumping from 40% to over 90%.

> The school leader explained to me that they had not made any other changes in the school; they simply started teaching all students in the school higher level mathematics. The students, receiving such a positive message and opportunity, responded fantastically, stepping up to learn the higher-level content and giving themselves the possibility of a much brighter future.
>
> *(Boaler, 2016)*

Teachers from St. Marylebone School in London recently moved to mixed ability teaching for ages 12–14 after two teachers from a school in Shanghai taught mathematics there for two weeks. To accommodate these teachers, who would only teach mixed ability, all 12-year-old students were moved into mixed ability classes where before they had been organized by current achievement level. The teachers decided to continue this practice for 13- and 14-year-olds because of the positive impact they saw. The mathematics team meets weekly for collaborative planning meetings, which have proved to be invaluable in shaping lessons. Any dialogue between teachers about the nitty gritty substance of learning, as happens for these teachers, provides fantastic professional development opportunities. Both for students and teachers, collaboration is at the top of the list of effect sizes for influences on learning.

Random pairing

The popular strategy of teachers organizing students with random learning partners, changing regularly (usually weekly in elementary/primary and every three lessons in secondary) is widely practiced in many schools and creates instant mixed ability. Students sit with a randomly chosen student as their 'talk partner' but might be doing different leveled work. The task is differentiated, not the students, and the damaging labeling of students grouped, set or tracked is avoided. In fact, the differences between students become 'a gift' with this strategy. In mathematics, it gives students an opportunity to see and talk about the mathematics topic in different contexts and in any writing activities peer discussions focusing on success and improvement are often enhanced by each other's ideas. Because of the regular change, students have a wide range of both cognitive and social pairings throughout the year. Instead of being placed by the teacher or always sitting with the same students, they have to adapt to every new pairing and avoid being cast as 'the helper' or 'helpee' or any other role when the seating arrangement rarely changes. One week they might be the higher achiever, helping and coaching the lower achiever, in another they could be the lower achiever, learning from a higher achiever. When students change their seating and therefore talk partner regularly, they are constantly learning in mixed ability groups, learning from each other. More detail and practical advice about this strategy can be found in 'Outstanding Formative Assessment' (Clarke, 2014).

Comments from students in schools in Clarke's learning teams 2016 about the value of random talk partners and the use of named popsicle/lolly sticks, with a summary of the strategy first:

The students sit randomly (usually determined by a computer randomiser program). After the teacher asks the class a question, the pairs are asked to discuss for 30 seconds or more together. The teacher has a pot of popsicle sticks with the students' names on them and, after the discussion time is up, chooses a stick randomly from the pot to determine which pair of students will respond to the question. This eliminates the 'hands up' culture, in which the same children tend to be first with their hands up leading to many children opting out of the thinking.

I think talk time is good because it gives us time to get a clear answer in our heads. And named lollysticks are good because everyone gets a go at answering
I enjoy the randomness of the popsicle sticks since you can't just be off the ball. So you try to concentrate because there is always a chance you'll get picked. I also like having the partners so you can find out the answer before the teacher asks.

I like having lollysticks because the people who always put their hands up don't always get picked. I also like to talk to a partner because you learn from them as well as the teacher.

Talk time is a great example of a good partnership and it really helps my learning seeing my partner's opinion. Popsicle sticks are really interesting because you never know if you are going to get picked.

The jigsaw strategy

One of the more powerful forms of creating mixed grouping is via the Jigsaw method, which has an effect size of 1.09. Just as in a jigsaw puzzle, each piece – each student's part – is essential for the completion and full understanding of the final product. If each student's part is essential, then each student is essential, and that is precisely what makes the strategy so effective (see www.jigsaw.org/overview.htm). To illustrate one way that Jigsaw can be used, imagine a task where we have five readings based on five influences from the Visible Learning book (a task we often use in our own workshops):

1. Sit at tables of about 3–5. Agree who is A, B, C, D and E.
2. Person A on each table reads and makes notes on one of the influences (e.g. classroom discussion); Bs do the same for teacher clarity; Cs on collaborative grouping, Ds on direct instruction and Es on class size. All have about 12 minutes.
3. All the As then meet together, similarly the Bs, Cs, Ds and Es to talk about the underlying issues and the main messages (about 15–20 minutes). The value here is that all students, regardless of their perceived ability, can teach and learn from each other about the content and ideas for each influence.
4. The students then return to their original groups and report back the major findings and understandings to the others. So now there are five sets of ideas and understandings for each group. The major purpose of this step is to see connections between the major ideas across the five influences.
5. Each group shares their major ideas and a whole class discussion is held to ensure that all understand the main themes underlying these five practices.

With this method mixed grouping is desirable, as students can become teachers and learners together, there is support for those who might struggle or sit back and not engage, and there are clear expectations for students' involvement throughout. Moreover, there are multiple opportunities to seek and receive feedback from peers.

Mixed ability teaching and mathematics

The issue of teaching mixed ability appears to be a particular issue in the teaching of mathematics, so it is worth exploring some solutions to the teaching of mixed ability before moving on to specific feedback issues. Giving every student the chance to succeed at mathematics must surely be the first step before we examine the most effective feedback.

Jo Boaler's 'Youcubed' website and her books 'The Elephant in the Classroom' (2008) and 'Mathematical Mindsets' (2016) describe mixed ability classes in which mathematics is explored with all children in an investigative yet rigorous style with outstanding achievement results. An example Boaler gives of a 'low floor high ceiling' mathematics task for secondary students:

What is the largest enclosure that can be made with 36, 1-metre pieces of fencing?

Students in one class experimented with rectangles, squares and triangles, then two students realized that the largest area came from a 36-sided shape (almost a circle). The teacher was able to introduce the two to the sine function to give them the height of each triangle made so that they could calculate the area of the shape.

Another popular strategy is to offer differentiated challenge choices to students sitting with random talk partners and therefore in mixed ability pairs. The choices are all on one sheet of paper so that students can move from one task to another if they find, after a while, that they are not in the learning zone (or zone of proximal development) because the task is too easy or too challenging. A key feature of these challenges is that they **all** contain a few practice items and application through problem solving or investigation but at different levels of difficulty **and all are focused around the same success criteria and learning intention.** What does not work is to make the easiest challenge simply practice, the middle challenge half practice and half problems and the hardest challenge all problem solving. All students need all elements and should not be marginalized from opportunities to problem solve and investigate, taking them into deeper learning and transfer of skills. More information can be found in Mathematical Mindsets and challenge choices are described in detail in 'Outstanding Formative Assessment' (Clarke, 2014). This revolution in the teaching of mathematics, especially, is well overdue.

f) Feedback and praise about the learning do not go together – but we like praise!

Students are, of course, human like all of us, and we all like to be praised. Praise can mean we are valued, it can mean the other person likes something about us or it can be affirmation that the task is complete. We often recall such praise although it is rarely rated as effective for improving performance (Lipnevich & Smith, 2008). Praise can also interfere with feedback about learning – if for no other reason than that we are inclined to remember the praise more than the feedback about the learning. When we refer to praise, we mean commendations about the student's worth, an expression of approval or admiration – most often directed at the person or student accomplishing some product or performance. This is quite different from 'positive reinforcement', which involves positive comments about a task, not the person.

Praise junkies

Care is needed, however, to not over-praise as it can give the message that the student is not capable (the perception being that the teacher gives more praise to lower achievers in the class to boost their confidence), and that the teacher has low expectations for the work of the over-praised student. Praise, also, can undermine resilience, as it sends messages that it is the student rather than their involvement and persistence in learning that determines success. Some students become praise junkies as their view of themselves is confirmed, independent of their performance and learning. They seek the praise, often independent of the quality of their learning. Typically, these praise junkies seek positive commendations to confirm their self-esteem and look acceptable in front of their peers. They risk not getting praise if they tackle challenging tasks where they might make errors.

Another problem with praise is that if it is given often, and therefore expected by students, its absence gives the message that the student is not worthy and can then lead to helplessness in the face of challenging tasks. If we watch closely those students who depend on praise, they have more eye checks with the teacher, are more interested in social comparison with their peers and are less likely to tackle tasks outside their zone of current achievement, for fear of not receiving praise. They dare not be wrong, dare not be challenged and dare not fail! Students should not engage in their learning contingent upon praise from adults rather than engage for the sheer enjoyment or fulfillment of learning.

Praise effects

Skipper and Douglas (2012), demonstrated that, when compared to 'no praise', students in praise conditions showed a more negative response to a single failure.

Ryan et al. (1983), in their meta-analysis, found that no form of praise is effective if it is given to encourage desired behavior, as described below:

Praise type	Effect size
Given for something other than engaging in the target activity (e.g. being helpful)	−0.14
Given for completing the activity	−0.39
Given for performing the activity well against various criteria	−0.44
Given for engaging but not necessarily completing the task	−0.28

These minus effect sizes are startling. So often person praise is directed to factors that the student has little control over such as their current achievement or perceived intelligence (e.g. 'You are so smart') and such praise can lead to a pattern of helplessness when faced with later failure compared to those who had been given feedback without such praise (Kamins & Dweck, 1999). Interestingly, the majority of students (69%) prefer any praise to be private or not receive praise at all (17%) (Burnett & Mandel, 2010; Merrett & Tang, 1994). This is probably because most praise is directed at students who the teacher perceives to be 'low ability' whereas most criticism is directed at those who the teacher perceives as 'high ability' (Meyer et al., 1986).

Effort praise
Praise about effort can also be harmful, as it can be interpreted as signifying a lack of ability, particularly for those students who see an inverse relation between effort and ability. For those who aim for mastery, effort praise can be demotivating and can lead to overdependence on comparison with other students, and less perseverance when faced with setbacks. Other students see praise for effort as a sign of their lack of intelligence, as they view those students who put in a lot of effort as a sign of low ability, as there is a general perception that lower achievers have to 'work harder' to attain the same results as higher achievers. Ask any adolescent in your school, 'Who is the "best learner"?' and often they say it is the person who gets everything completed quickly, does not have to expend energy and work hard, and just knows it all! This is the very opposite of a great learner. The effect of praise for effort is rarely positive. Carol Dweck adds:

> A lot of teachers say praise the effort, not the outcome. Teachers were praising effort that was not effective, saying 'Wow, you tried really hard!' But students know that if they didn't make progress and you're praising them, it's a consolation prize. They also know you think they can't do any better. I say praise the effort that led to the outcome or learning progress: tie the praise to it. It's not just effort but strategy. Students need to know that if they're stuck, they don't need just effort. You don't want them redoubling their efforts with the same ineffective strategies.
> *(Dweck, 2016)*

Praise helps build relations

In a study by Cohen and Garcia (2014), hundreds of high school English class students wrote essays and received diagnostic comments from their teachers. Half the students received one more sentence: *'I am giving you this feedback because I believe in you'*. The students who received this message achieved at significantly higher levels a year later even though the teachers did not know who had received the sentence and there were no other differences between the groups. This emphasizes the power of the words teachers use in the classroom, many of which convey the beliefs, expectations and personal feelings towards their students. Words given by teachers have the potential to be remembered, either positively or negatively, for a lifetime.

Praise: the bottom line

The above message is simple: do not mix feedback about the learning with praise, as the praise will interfere with and dilute the message about learning.

> To employ praise in the belief or in the confidence that a student will be made thus to react, or to produce, maximally, is to proceed upon false assumptions, to build on a foundation of clay.
>
> *(Schmidt, 1941)*

Such praise moves attention away from the learning (Kluger & DeNisi, 1996), but there is every reason we can and should praise students – it can help build relations and trust. Praise unrelated to a task might be welcomed if used sparingly, and should be specific, sincere, accurate, earned, preferably unexpected, not exaggerated or contrived, more private than public, not include social comparison and not a generalized set of approvals *(e.g. 'I'm proud of the way you stood up for yourself at that moment. You were polite but made it clear you were not going to stand for it. Well done')*.

g) External rewards as negative feedback

The evidence

Programed instruction, praise, punishment and extrinsic rewards were the least effective forms of feedback for enhancing achievement. Indeed, it is doubtful whether rewards should be thought of as feedback at all. Deci, Koestner and Ryan (1999) have described tangible rewards (stickers, awards and so on) as contingencies to activities rather than feedback because they contain so little task information. In their meta-analysis of the effects of feedback on motivation, these authors found a negative correlation between extrinsic rewards and task performance (-0.34). Extrinsic rewards are a controlling strategy that often leads to greater surveillance, evaluation and competition, all of which have been found to undermine enhanced engagement and regulation (Deci & Ryan, 1985).

(Hattie, 2009)

Many studies (e.g. Dweck, 1989; Elliot & Dweck, 1988) show that performance goals such as stickers etc. lead to students who:

- avoid challenge when they have doubts about their ability compared with others,
- tend to create an excuse for failure,
- concentrate much of their task analysis on gauging the difficulty of the task and calculating the chances of gaining favorable ability judgments,
- attribute difficulty to low ability,
- give up in the face of difficulty,
- become upset when faced with difficulty or failure.

Lepper and Hodell (1989) found that external rewards have a detrimental effect on intrinsic motivation. When seeking extrinsic rewards, students are encouraged to complete tasks as quickly as possible and include only those features which will get them the reward. Intrinsic motivation, on the other hand, in which the learning itself is the reward, and achievement is verbalized, leads to more effective, deeper and longer lasting learning.

External rewards have the same impact as grades which do not include interpretive feedback – encouraging students to take notice only of their grade/reward in comparison to others (*Have I got a reward? Did I do better than others?*), to become complacent if they receive consistently high grades or rewards (*I'm so smart I don't need to push myself*) and to become demoralized when grades are consistently low or rewards are rare (*I'm no good at this – why should I bother?*).

One of the most significant passages in Black and Wiliam's 'Inside the black box' digest of their 1998 review reads:

> Where the classroom culture focuses on rewards, gold stars, grades or place in the class rankings, then students look for the ways to obtain the best marks rather than at the needs of their learning which these marks ought to reflect. One reported consequence is that where they have any choice, students avoid difficult tasks. They also spend time and energy looking for clues to the 'right answer'. Many are reluctant to ask questions out of fear of failure. Students who encounter difficulties and poor results are led to believe that they lack ability, and this belief leads them to attribute their difficulties to a defect in themselves about which they cannot do a great deal. So they 'retire hurt', avoid investing effort in learning which could only lead to disappointment and try to build up their self-esteem in other ways. Whilst the higher achievers can do well in such a culture, the overall effect is to enhance the frequency and the extent of underachievement.

Feedback to any student should be about the particular qualities of his or her work, with advice on what he or she can do to improve, and should avoid comparisons with other students.

(Black & Wiliam, 1998b)

If students and teachers are focused around learning intentions, success criteria, challenging themselves, celebrating success and striving for improvement, rewards become unnecessary, patronizing and distracting. Instead, students and teachers privilege the desire to learn by verbally celebrating achievement and struggle, as they are continually aware of the only reward that matters – the gift of learning.

Key points

- Feedback is part of the formative assessment/evaluation framework: learning intentions, co-constructed success criteria, knowing what good examples look like, effective questioning and effective feedback.
- The skill, will and thrill: effective learning and therefore effective feedback needs the skills students bring to the task, the understanding and ability to apply learning dispositions to it, and excitement and curiosity in learning.
- Mindsets and mindframes: we aim for students to think with growth not fixed mindsets when they are challenged or do not know what to do next. Such mindframes involve them knowing how to learn, how to speak about learning, feeling responsible for enhancing their learning and collaborating with others in this learning.
- Errors are opportunities for learning and should not be treated as something to be avoided or signs of failure.
- Mixed ability is a prerequisite for maximizing teacher and student expectations and achievement and can lead to higher levels of feedback among students.
- While praise can help create trust and positive relationships, do not mix praise and feedback about the learning. Praise can detract from investment in learning.
- There is a negative correlation between external rewards and task performance. Feedback in all forms should avoid comparisons with other students.

3

Teaching and learning frameworks

So far, we have looked at how feedback has evolved and the ideal feedback culture. We now focus on the teaching and learning structures which we believe give the best possible framework for feedback, in any direction, to be effective: 1) Prior knowledge lesson starters, 2) Sharing learning intentions, 3) Co-constructing success criteria and 4) The use of the stages of the SOLO taxonomy.

The learning cycle, shown in Figure 3.1, describes the most common place and time for these structures, but, because learning is a winding journey, filled with remembering then forgetting, the stages are merely a framework for facilitating, rather than dictating, that journey.

1. Prior knowledge lesson starters

Ausubel's point about the significance of prior knowledge in determining what should be taught (and therefore more accurately focusing feedback for that learning) is worth noting:

> The most important single factor influencing learning is what the learner already knows. Ascertain this and teach him accordingly.
>
> *(Ausubel, 1968)*

Avoid disconnects

When time is short, and coverage is great, it can be tempting to miss out the introduction of a prior knowledge discussion starter and to hit the ground running with one's lesson plan. Disconnects often occur when current understanding has not first been investigated. Students might not have remembered and therefore not deeply understood yesterday's learning, or, in the other direction, they might be able to demonstrate understanding beyond the teacher's expectation. Either way, the lesson plan often needs to be adjusted, usually during the lesson when these elements are

Figure 3.1 The cycle of learning

revealed. Worse, boredom or lack of understanding can create behavior problems and exacerbate the issue. The most important factor at lessons starts is that teachers need to be open to feedback from students about what they already know or do not know.

We need to also note that too often we presume students do not know the material for the next lesson. Nuthall (2005) found that about 50–60% of material taught in a lesson is already known by the students. Maybe this is taking scaffolding too far!

Two things need to happen:

1) It is unwise to over-plan lessons, making the teacher duty bound to plough through the activities regardless of student understanding. Instead, the bare bones learning intentions and mechanisms for co-constructing success criteria,

as well as any planned prior knowledge question, resources and so on, allow for changing direction at any time.

2) A five-minute (or thereabouts) prior knowledge discussion question or activity, reflecting the subject matter of the lesson, has multiple benefits: students are instantly engaged in discussing and reflecting on their current understanding of the lesson focus; the teacher can listen to conversations and gauge current level of understanding; decisions can be made about how the planned lesson should proceed. As with many aspects covered in this chapter, time spent on prior knowledge is an investment which saves time in the long run.

The following starter question templates are examples successfully used by teachers. Some can be developed and built on whereas others simply set the theme for the lesson and give prior knowledge a chance to be revealed – valuable feedback from student to teacher. The starter question focuses the student to be able to recognize and reveal how much they already know about the content, beginning the process of self-assessment at the very start of a lesson.

Question template	Example	Example	Example
Range of answers	What is 5 squared? Discuss these 'answers' and give possible reasons for the wrong ones: 3, 7, 10, 25, 125	Which physical activities improve the efficiency of the heart? Discuss: cycling, walking, golf, swimming, skydiving, darts	Which strategies are likely to persuade? Discuss: evidence, bias, empathy, bullying, objectivity, bribery
Statement	Friction is always useful. Agree or disagree? Say why . . .	Goldilocks was a burglar. Agree or disagree? Say why . . .	45% of 365 is greater than 54% of 285. Agree or disagree? Say why . . .
Odd one out	Which of these is odd? 1/2 25/50 1/3 3/6 Say why . . .	Which of these is odd? Slowly, carefully, bright, happily Say why . . .	Which of these is odd? Nuts, meat, eggs, lettuce, fish
What went wrong?	'Look! Said Alice, 'There goes the white rabbit! Discuss . . .	(Picture of a circuit not connected properly) Discuss . . .	$18 \times 5 = 10 \times 5 + 9 \times 5$ $= 50 + 45$ $= 95$ Discuss . . .
Explain to another student . . .	how you know that 1/3 is bigger than 1/4.	the difference between a simile and a metaphor.	how photosynthesis happens.

One teacher in a learning team of teachers experimenting with prior knowledge discussion starters used the following examples at the beginnings of lessons with her class:

> How are decimals like whole numbers and how are they different? (Math)
>
> Does sentence start variety play a more important part in fiction or non-fiction? (English)
>
> Which other era that you've learnt about do the Mayans remind you most of and why? (History)
>
> What were the three hardest decisions Vorjak had to make so far? (English)

Students gave the following responses about the value of prior knowledge discussion starters. Although the purpose, from the teacher's point of view, is to gain feedback from the students about what they already know or think, some of the students make explicit reference to the fact that they are also learning through the discussions:

> I feel those type of questions are better because you can go into more depth when talking to your partner.
>
> I like open questions, because it helps me think and talk to my partner. I like listening to other people's answers and reasons.
>
> I like questions when you don't straight away know the answer and you have to talk to your partner.
>
> It deepens my understanding in simple things. I also like generating ideas with a partner and having a proper discussion about it.
>
> Having open questions really deepens my learning and makes me understand about the subject of the question. This is a really good way for me to learn.

Act on the feedback

As with feedback given to students, the issue is whether feedback is understood and then acted upon. Prior knowledge starters give feedback information *from student to teacher*. How and whether the teacher reacts to this is the key question. Simply covering misunderstood concepts again in the same way is clearly unadvisable but asking students to pair up and become learning detectives and learning coaches for one another or asking for volunteer students to be teacher at the front are strategies which use the students as learning resources for one another and can be more effective than teachers seeing themselves as the only teachers. Discovering that some of the teacher's planned activities are unnecessary means the teacher can aim higher, focusing on consolidating or applying previous learning – going deeper.

Gary Wilkie, school leader from Sheringham School, shared his thoughts about feedback and gave an example of effective feedback related to the teacher he witnessed:

Feedback is an incredibly important part of what I am now calling 'the learning dialogue' but I wonder how often feedback is 'done properly' and how often it is part of the formative assessment cycle. I'm not overly convinced that written feedback on one piece of work makes a difference and oral feedback is fantastic, but surely less effective if that feedback isn't informing the teacher's next step as much as it is the student's.

The best example of feedback I have seen recently was when I was engaged in a collaborative enquiry of teaching. This process involves a pre-meet with the teachers before a lesson, talking to them about their aspirations for learning within the lesson, observing the lesson, then having a genuine dialogue with them about what went well. In this particular pre-conversation, the teacher talked about how the lesson they were about to teach was radically different from the one they had planned in the sequence of lessons. It had become clear to her from the student outcomes and conversations with the students that they were insecure about finding 10% of a number, so the planned lessons about cumulative percentage increases needed to be amended with more practical apparatus and real life examples, ensuring that students understood the concept and therefore find the algorithm easier to remember. As part of the amended lesson, the teacher fed back to the students what they had done well yesterday and explicitly applied it to the new context they were working on as a key concept. The lesson I saw was very successful.

(Gary Wilkie, Sheringham School)

2. Sharing learning intentions

Sharing learning intentions is a fundamental requirement both for learning and feedback (Sadler, 1989). Without it students have no idea how they will be evaluated, and their task becomes a matter of finding out or guessing what the teacher wants them to do, rather than engaging with the activity and its learning goals.

If I am asked to paint a rainbow, for instance, without the learning intention, I have no idea upon which criteria my work will be assessed, or what is in the teacher's mind. If I am told that we are learning to blend colors, on the other hand, the whole lesson focus will be about this skill and therefore my purpose and focus would be clear. Another reason for sharing learning intentions is that the skill in hand can be seen in its wider setting, and therefore the potential for its application. I once watched a teacher, for example, tell the students that they were learning about the journey of a banana. Her real intention was for them to understand the extraction of resources, and she had chosen this example to teach the concept. The real intention was never mentioned, however, so the children's experience was to know only how bananas get from their place of origin to our country. If she had, on the other hand, explained that the learning intention was the extraction of resources, or how different products get from one place to another, the students could have brainstormed with her different resources that are found, packaged and then travel from one place to another. The journey of a banana, therefore, now becomes just one of any possible journeys which could be explored, and the students now see its place and the possibilities for other resources. Knowing core learning intentions rather than just the activity allows for greater application and understanding. As success criteria are a breakdown of the learning intention *(What do you have to do to achieve this?)*, knowing the exact skill involved makes the process of teacher/student co-construction clearer and easier, as illustrated in the next few pages.

The learning intention focuses the teacher thus:

What do I want them to learn (not do – an important distinction)?
How do I articulate that, what would be a good way of learning it?
What do I think a range of excellent finished products would look like?

Feedback should first and foremost link with the learning intention and success criteria of the lesson, although many other classroom factors, such as social and metacognitive elements, and unexpected excellence not linked to those features clearly also demand feedback from teacher to student as well as student to student and student to teacher.

When to share learning intentions

Writing the learning intention on the white board before the lesson begins might be appropriate for some lessons, but for others might kill student interest before the lesson begins. Bearing in mind the importance of prior knowledge starters, it is often the case that the prior knowledge discussion reveals to students the intended learning intention.

The bottom line for the timing of when to share learning intentions is that *it must be known if not knowing it would affect student performance and therefore any evaluation made by the teacher.*

Sometimes an overarching learning intention is then broken down over several days into aspects of the processes involved. In a series of lessons about writing balanced arguments (a key writing skill, involving arguing for and against), for instance, the learning journey through the week might look like this:

Learning journey: Balanced argument

1. Analyze examples of good and poor balanced arguments.
2. Create success criteria and look for them, as a class, in examples of old student work.
3. Write whole class balanced argument – edit-improve.
4. Write own balanced arguments/self/peer improvements.

This 'big picture' helps students see the progression of learning. Knowing how each part of the jigsaw fits together in advance is a secret we have often not let students into, something adults would be unlikely to tolerate. Imagine how motivation would be impacted if we were to start a set of art lessons, for instance, or attend a day's course with no agenda, having no idea about the content of each session. Apart from the motivation impact, not knowing the big picture makes it much harder to place each piece of learning into the whole as it is happening. SOLO is also a useful tool for displaying the mental models involved in the progression of a learning journey, as described on page 69.

What should learning intentions look like?

Credible

Learning intentions need to be credible to the students, reflect what is really going to be taught or learnt for that lesson and specific, but not necessarily over precise. A series of lessons getting to know the play 'Romeo and Juliet' for instance would probably have a different learning intention for each lesson, even if each is a breakdown of the overarching main objective for all the lessons. Ask any teacher 'What did you really want them to learn for that lesson?' and it is highly likely that they will have a fairly specific answer. That answer is usually the exact learning intention the students should be given.

Decontextualized

Learning intentions need to be decontextualized if the context is not central to the skill. So learning **to design a poster for a holiday in St Lucia** is not a transferrable learning intention, whereas learning how **to design a poster** is transferable to both different contexts and different subjects. Of course students will know and will discuss the context for this lesson as a travel poster or a School Fair poster, but pointing out all the different *possible* contexts helps the student see the central generic skill being learnt. Another vital reason for decontextualizing learning intentions is that the subsequent success criteria need to be equally unmuddied by the context so that they can be usefully transferred. If we were to break down the contextualized, and therefore inappropriate, learning intention the success criteria might look like this:

How not to do it! Contextualized learning intention ...

We are learning to design a poster for a holiday to St Lucia

Remember to include:
- *A picture of the beach*
- *A picture of the accommodation*
- *Information about St Lucia*
- *Persuasive language*
- *Value for money of the holiday*
- *Clear lettering about the destination*

DON'T DO THIS!

The learning intention contains the context – so would work for this lesson only. The features here would be discussed of course, and highlighted for this lesson, but as activity steps rather than success criteria which are most effective as a breakdown of the skill rather than activity instructions.

Once learning intentions become decontextualized with a core skill as the focus, the co-constructing of success criteria becomes meaningful. For this lesson, then, it would be useful, perhaps, to show the class an excellent poster from last year's class, alongside one which was not so good. Asking for learning partner discussions would not only reveal students' prior knowledge, but also engage them immediately in determining why poster A is better than Poster B. Asking for their responses and recording the features the best poster has effectively generates the success criteria for poster design. You might expect to see the following:

How to do it! Decontextualized learning intention

We are learning to design an effective poster

Remember to include:
- *Clear, large lettering*
- *Important information (e.g. cost, dates and times)*
- *Eye-catching, relevant pictures*
- *Colors which stand out against the background*
- *Persuasive hook*

BETTER!

The learning intention is now a pure skill, so the criteria can be transferred to the creation of any poster.

How many learning intentions? (Knowledge and skills)

Although there is usually one learning intention for a lesson (the main focus for the learning), there are often two forms of learning intentions at play: the knowledge you want them to acquire and the skill they will use either in acquiring that knowledge or in applying it. Both learning intentions need to be known, at the appropriate time, but the skill-based learning intention will be the one which has accompanying process success criteria. Knowledge acquisition is vital for the development of skills, also providing engaging and stimulating contexts, but the breakdown of knowledge is better placed in curriculum planning than in success criteria. Skills set us up to be able to apply them in life situations in any context and to be able to learn anything we want to, again in any context. The point is to feedforward information to the student about the purposes of their learning, so that they can become complicit in this learning cycle. So, **knowledge** learning intentions might look like this:

To know the key events of the Iraq War
To know the terms longitude and latitude
To know properties of 3D shapes
To know the reasons for the American Civil War

These objectives imply information giving or researching, but we want students to not only know these objectives, but also to be able to use them when they are practicing or exploring skills. Rarely is information just given to students. We usually ask them to do something with that knowledge, present it in some way or use it in tandem with another skill, often from another subject domain (e.g. Literacy). **Possible skills** which would be linked with these knowledge learning objectives might be:

To know the key events of the Iraq War + **To be able to write a diary (context: a refugee)**

To know the terms longitude and latitude + **To be able to write an explanation text**

To know properties of 3D shapes + **To be able to use a Venn diagram**

To know the reasons for the American Civil War + **To be able to use sources to distinguish between fact and opinion**

Thus, both learning intentions would be displayed, but only the skill would usefully have associated success criteria, which, as a breakdown of the learning intention, break the skill down into its component parts or possible ingredients.

Writing the learning intention in students' books – worth it?

One of the least helpful practices pushed upon many teachers is that they should have learning intentions written in every student's book for every piece of work. While a fluent writer might quickly write this as the title of their work when any writing is required, many teachers spend valuable preparation time cutting and pasting typed learning intentions into young students' books in order to be more accountable and to prove that they know what they are doing. The tension between accountability and student learning has always existed and, in our opinion, needs courage among school leaders to make clear that all practices in the school have only one aim – to further student learning. 'Know thy impact' is at the heart of this of course, because, if you can show that by spending more time on planning, the result is that the learning improves, or that by spending planning time writing in students' books the learning is diminished, then the course of action is clear.

3. Success criteria

Royce Sadler's 'closing the gap' three-part criteria has, as its first, the following necessary stage in becoming an effective learner:

Possesses a concept of the standard (or goal, or reference level) being aimed for.
(Sadler, 1989)

We have previously outlined the importance of students knowing the learning intention, but, in order to possess a 'concept' of this intention, more needs to happen. Success criteria (effect size 1.13), as well as the analysis of good examples of the finished product, help to build this 'concept'. Success criteria have evolved over the last 20 years, so, to understand the current thinking about their form, a little history is useful . . .

The history of the development of success criteria

When the National Curriculum was introduced into the UK in 1989, learning intentions became statutory coverage for all teachers. Once teachers had got their heads around what learning intentions for lessons should look like, and how they should be presented to students, the next step, naturally evolving, was the advent of success criteria – what would a student have to do to achieve success for this piece of work, in order to fulfil the learning intention?

To begin with, success criteria tended to be product based (e.g. by the end, you will have written two paragraphs). This told students nothing about how to achieve this. There also emerged success criteria which were the basic activity steps involved in a task, something every task needs, but usually linked more to the context than the learning intention (e.g. first cut out the pictures, then stick them in order on the butterfly sheet, then color them in, remembering the correct colors). It was when we discovered that if success criteria were a breakdown of the decontextualized or pure skill involved and focused on the process, rather than product expectations or task steps, the improvement in learning was revealed. The Gillingham Evaluation Study (Clarke, 2001) concluded that where teachers were creating *process* based success criteria linked with a decontextualized skill (e.g. You need to remember to include the following . . .), focusing on what needed to be done during the process, learning was more effective. A link was also noticed between these and American 'rubrics'. Clarke's work with teachers evaluating formative assessment strategies over seventeen years has enabled a picture of the different types and functions of success criteria which maximize learning. Learning intentions tend to be either:

a) closed (as in grammar, punctuation, math procedures – right or wrong) with equally closed and compulsory success criteria (remember to . . .) which are the rules or steps to follow or,

b) open (as in story structure, narrative writing, art-quality difficult to quantify) with a menu of possible items to include, optional rather than compulsory.

So success criteria are simply a breakdown of the learning intention and provide a benchmark for the quality of the learning. The concept of the intention becomes complete when examples of the goal in real terms (i.e. the finished product) are shown, analyzed or developed. When the success criteria are **co-constructed** with the students, rather than simply given to them, students have a still greater chance of understanding and internalizing their meanings and 'possessing a concept of the goal'.

Once the learner has success criteria they have a framework for a formative dialogue, with peers or adults, which enable them to:

- know what the learning objective means,
- know the compulsory steps involved with a closed learning objective (e.g. to find percentages of whole numbers) or the elements of a particular writing form (e.g. a newspaper report),
- know the possible ingredients for an open learning objective (e.g. a ghost story opening),
- identify where success has been achieved and where help might be needed,
- be clearer about where improvements can be made,
- discuss strategies for improvement,
- reflect on progress.

Two types of success criteria linked to closed and open learning intentions

Success criteria can either be *a) compulsory elements* as in this example:

> Learning intention: **to use inverted commas**
>
> *You will be successful when you*
>
> - *start each new person's speech on a new line,*
> - *put speech marks before and after speech,*
> - *put full stops, exclamation marks etc. before the final speech mark.*

or b) *a menu of possible inclusions* as in the following:

> Learning intention: to write a story which uses **suspense**
>
> *Choose from*
>
> - *show not tell (e.g. 'The hair on the back of her neck stood up' rather than 'She was scared'),*
> - *short sentences to build suspense (e.g. 'It crept towards me. Slowly. Menacingly'),*
> - *keep some things secret or unrevealed (e.g. 'She could hear something scratching'),*
> - *place any characters in scary settings (e.g. alone/in the dark).*

The first success criteria *(compulsory elements in closed learning intentions)* are features of surface learning, equipping the learner for more complex tasks. The second set of success criteria (*possible inclusions for open learning intentions*) are examples of deeper learning, in which previous learning is retrieved, consolidated and applied.

The two main types of learning intentions and their subsequent success criteria can be described as **closed and open or rules and tools.** The simplest learning intentions are the specific, closed skills which have compulsory elements and usually need to be learnt or memorized. As long as these rules are followed correctly, attainment will be the same for all students – quality is not an issue. Put simply, if the goal is to be able to use commas correctly, and all the criteria have been correctly attained, then attainment is equal for all students for that learning intention. There can be no debate about whose commas are best, for instance! More complex are the success criteria for open learning intentions, which, through analysis of good examples, consist of a menu of possible inclusions. We cannot dictate exactly which criteria a student should choose to use in a characterization, for instance, because each student's writing will be unique and will be judged on the quality of their writing as well as the inclusion of any success criteria, although some teachers highlight some of the success criteria if they definitely want students to focus on those for that lesson. Success criteria can provide clear feedback to the student about where they are going in their learning.

Both types of learning intentions, their subsequent success criteria and implications for feedback are now explored.

Type A: Compulsory success criteria: RULES

Examples of *closed learning intentions with compulsory success criteria (rules)*

We are learning to . . .

Use capital letters and full stops *(success criteria: capital letters are used at the beginning of sentences, titles and names of people and places; full stops are placed at ends of sentences; exclamation marks and question marks act as full stops)*

To use the column method of addition
To be able to use inverted commas
To simplify equations
To be able to construct a bar graph
To be able to use a Bunsen burner
To identify colors in German
To partition numbers
To simplify brackets used in algebra

Non-fiction writing learning intentions also come under the 'rules' category although, unlike those above, they do not guarantee quality.

Examples of *non-fiction writing intentions (rules)*:

We are learning to . . .

Write a letter *(success criteria: address is on the right-hand side at the top; the date goes under the address; Choose formal or informal beginning – Dear Mr. Smith or Dear Dad; write the letter under the Dear . . .; Choose an appropriate sign off from the class list)*

Write persuasively
Write a reasoned argument
Write a newspaper article
Write instructions

Each of these has a set of success criteria which lay out the compulsory structure of the writing type. A newspaper article, for example, must have a headline, a sub-heading, the journalist's name and so on, because this is the conventional structure. Once writing is included in the structure, however, quality becomes an issue and the inclusion of the success criteria alone does not guarantee excellence. Quality is drawn from a variety of sources, such as the student's own reading and, significantly, how many examples of 'good ones' have been analyzed by the class before and during their own individual attempts.

Implications for feedback

In the first examples above (*closed learning intentions with compulsory criteria*) feedback can effectively focus around the criteria. The criteria must be followed for the learning intention to be fulfilled so feedback needs to give advice about any criteria not fulfilled. With closed criteria and a closed learning intention (*e.g. steps in a mathematical procedure or rules for a particular punctuation rule*) feedback is often little more than a reminder of the rule and encouragement to keep practicing it. Clearly if there is a lack of understanding at any point then the feedback needs to focus on what appears to be the stumbling block – involving instant diagnosis. If a step in a mathematical procedure keeps going wrong, for instance, and there is clearly a place value misconception, there is no point continuing with the procedure until the place value understanding is developed.

In the second, non-fiction writing examples above, however, feedback has two main functions:

1) Information about the inclusion or not of the compulsory elements which form the conventional **structure** of the text type (consolidation of surface learning).
2) Identification of 'successes' or best words or phrases used within the structure and advice about how the writing could be improved, the focus being on how well the piece is written (acquisition and consolidation of deep learning and transfer).

It is with this type of learning intention and its related success criteria that teachers often also point the students to 'Good writing' success criteria (see below for a typical example for students 9 years of age and over). Thus the students are using the first success criteria (To write a newspaper article) as a structural guide for their writing, and the second (What makes good writing) as their guide to make the piece as good as it can be. 'Good writing' success criteria are a summary of taught skills, relative to the age group of the students, as well as guidance about what is important in the writing process. They are usually seen as a poster in the classroom, because they are a common factor regardless of the subject learning intention, alongside 'Every time we write' criteria and 'Every time we do mathematics' criteria, both as posters. Every subject in secondary schools could, in fact, have a similar 'Every time we do . . .' poster, reminding students of elements they should always check for. These criteria make up a tool box for the consolidation, application and transfer of acquired skills. 'Every time we write', appropriate to the age of the students, would consist of, for 6-year-olds for instance, criteria such as leaving finger spaces between words and sounding out words, whereas for 14-year-olds the criteria would cover topics such as checking spelling and grammar and using PEE (*point, evidence, explain*). We can see, therefore, that success criteria can be fixed and compulsory or guidance for quality, either short term or long term. The following success criteria (What makes good writing) are intended to be in the form of a poster in the classroom which are referred to when students are writing – so that maybe only one or two would be referenced at a time. This is in contrast to success criteria which are co-constructed for a particular skill (e.g. instructional writing) and only used for those lessons.

What makes good writing? (Poster of ongoing success criteria in the form of questions)

- What effect do you want your writing to have on the reader?
- What will do this best? (e.g. dialogue/flashback/descriptive setting/significant event etc.)
- Have you avoided obvious clichéd descriptions in your writing?
- Have you made sure your adjectives tell the reader something they would not have known?
- Have you chosen interesting, informative nouns and verbs (e.g. 'the policeman stared at the golden eagle' rather than 'the man looked at the bird')?
- Have you shown the reader how characters feel and look rather than showing them?
- How do you want the reader to feel when they read your ending? Choose the best way of doing this.
- Could you include similes, metaphors, alliteration, adverbs, personification etc. if they improve the effect you want to create?

Type B: Choice success criteria: TOOLS

Open learning intentions are those usually concerned with some kind of narrative writing for any subject or topic, in which the same success criteria can be used across the class, but the finished products will vary in their quality, even if all the success criteria have been fulfilled. The writing suspense example used earlier is a good example:

Learning intention: **suspense writing**

Choose from:

- show not tell,
- use flashbacks,
- use ellipses,
- repeated words,
- keep some things secret or unrevealed,
- place any characters in scary settings (e.g. alone/in the dark).

A student might choose a number of these success criteria but still not have written something of the highest quality. Another student in the class might have used the same success criteria but ended up with a piece of writing of higher quality than the first student's. This is where success criteria have their limits. Although they give a toolkit of possibilities with open learning intentions, for writing assignments, they cannot ensure excellence. It is through students' exposure to good writing and reading and the analysis of these, as well as effective feedback which shows how and where to improve, that they are most likely to reach standards of excellence in their own writing.

Implications for feedback

One of the problems with focusing feedback only on success criteria in student writing is that we can find ourselves ignoring examples of excellence which do not match any of the success criteria. It is important to remember the point of narrative writing – the author's intent and the impact on the reader are the ultimate aims, with success criteria simply giving ideas and structure along the way. The following diary extract from a primary school student was a good example of the diary writing criteria being met, but the most compelling aspect of the writing was the student's use of the word 'sick' in various ways, not listed (of course!) in the success criteria:

> *So we went to San Diego Zoo in a sick seven seater bus (nice kind of sick)… my favorite animals were the lions, although one was doing its business behind the glass (the bad kind of sick) . . . On the way home I was ill in the bus and was sick (ok this time it's vomit).*

If we were to only focus on a student's use of success criteria we could lead them to believe that a good piece of writing can be identified only with those elements, rather than how it makes you feel or think.

As long as the basic structure of a student's writing has been consistent with the success criteria, the feedback is best focused on identifying any excellence, of any kind, so that these act as a guide to future writing and knowing what excellence looks like. With regular peer discussions over each other's writing, students can become highly skilled in identifying the 'best bits' in any writing and being able to articulate their reasons for the choice. Identification of excellence goes hand in hand with feedback about where or how any improvements can be made. Although this is covered in the next chapter, it is worth saying at this point that the most useful improvement suggestions give *explicit examples rather than woolly suggestions* and are focused around improvement to be made *on the current piece* rather than in any future venture, which would probably be in a completely different context and, because of the difficulty of transposing advice about one context to another and the time that has elapsed, more difficult to carry over.

Anecdote from English teacher of 13-year-olds
Learning intention: To analyze the conventions of ballads
During several lessons, students read and analyzed ballads – using a table to compare the similarities, differences and ballad conventions:

	Ballad 1	**Ballad 2**	**Ballad 3**
Story			
Moral			
Chorus			
Rhythm			
Rhyme			
Shape			

Doing this with three different ballads saw students remembering and recognizing common ballad conventions.

Students were unaware, whilst doing this, that they were building up success criteria for the next activity.

At the start of this lesson, students were told that they would learn to write in the style of a ballad. At this, students complained and groaned and they seemed apprehensive at such a mammoth task . . .

Students were given the first and last verses of *The Sad Story of Lefty and Ned* to work on. Students were asked, in pairs, to discuss the following questions:

1. *What do the first and last verses tell us about the two characters?*
2. *There is a chorus in the ballad. What is it? Where does it occur?*

3. *What is the rhyming pattern in the ballad?*
4. *How would you describe the rhythm of the ballad?*

These questions relate to the aspects covered in the ballads grid.

Students were then asked for the learning intention, context and success criteria. To form the success criteria, I asked students to think about their answers to the above questions and the conventions of the previous ballads. Students supplied these easily, confidently and were not afraid of contributing, making them feel good about their knowledge. Students copied the table to help them write their own version:

Learning intention	Context	Success criteria
To write a ballad	*The Sad Story of Lefty and Ned*	* Rhyme scheme: AABB * Rhythm: fast – 4 beats per line * Chorus: last 2 lines of verse * 4 lines per verse * 7 new verses

In pairs, students discussed possible storylines, which they shared with the class. Individually, students then planned their own story of Lefty and Ned as a flow-chart, which was used, with the success criteria, to write their ballad. After such a negative response, students had forgotten their doubts and were eager to get started. All were comfortable with the task and the success criteria. Much to their surprise, every student enjoyed it and the lesson ended on a high.

Students are no longer confused about the purpose of certain tasks or learning intentions. The co-construction of success criteria has improved students' self-esteem because they're able to contribute to class discussions and complete the work by following the success criteria. I believe that this heightened sense of self-efficacy has improved my rapport with my classes because there is less confrontation and more opportunity for positive feedback. Overall, students are more actively involved in lessons, having gained the ability to help their peers and participate in discussion. Students are more enthusiastic towards English as a result.

(Taken from Clarke, 2005)

Mathematics success criteria

As with most subjects, there are mathematical learning intentions focusing on closed skills which need to be consolidated, over-learnt and placed eventually in our long-term memory. Then there are mathematical calculations to be solved which require us to retrieve learnt strategies upon which we draw. *Deep learning and transfer* occurs when those skills can be applied to any context in which choices have to be made to achieve success. Success criteria reflect the kind of learning intention in hand, so a closed procedure with compulsory steps would probably have step by step success criteria; a calculation would have a choice of possible methods and a mathematical problem would have problem solving success criteria, as follows:

Closed success criteria for a specific skill (surface acquiring).	Open success criteria when students have learnt a range of techniques (surface consolidating).	Open success criteria which focus on problem solving processes and decision making (deep consolidating and transfer).
To add two-digit numbers by the column method.	*To add two-digit numbers.*	*To solve a word problem: how many hours have you been alive?*
Remember to: • add the units first, • carry any tens, • add the tens next, remembering any carried numbers.	**Choose from:** • a mental method, • using a number line, • the column method, • adding tens first, then units, then both together, • partitioning.	**Remember to:** • estimate the answer, • underline the key words, • choose a method, • choose resources, • change your strategy if it doesn't work, • check your answer a different way, • compare your answer with your estimate.

Anecdote from mathematics teacher of 16-year-olds

Introducing process success criteria has had a positive impact on my teaching and my students' learning in a short space of time. I use the terms 'instructions' or 'method to . . .' instead of 'process success criteria' to ensure my students understand what I'm talking about. Together we decide what the instructions should be whilst I demonstrate by example. They enjoy choosing words that they understand as this gives them a sense of ownership of the topic and the lesson.

The most successful examples of this have been with two higher-level topics: **standard deviation and comparative pie charts.** Students felt overwhelmed by the prospect of these lessons as they feared it might be out of their reach academically but having worked together to decide the instructions, they felt the work had become accessible to them.

As they used the instructions repeatedly to answer questions, some students began to realise why they were doing certain steps. Using the instructions was a base for understanding, not simply carrying out a method. I heard students saying:

'Oh, you square all the answers in step 2 because when you subtract the mean from each value, you get negative numbers . . . and you don't want to work with negative numbers, that's too hard'. (15-year-old)

'I'm not quite sure but when you divide the area of the first pie chart by how many it stands for, you get how much space one person represents. That's right because in step 3, you times it by how many people the second pie chart stands for and that gives you its area'.- (16-year-old)

. . . and my favourite,

'Ooooooh, I get it!' (16-year-old)

This change in student learning, awareness and interaction has had a significant impact on my role in the classroom. My students know what to do because it's in front of them and there has been a decrease in student-teacher interaction and them asking me for help as they ask each other). I have more time to watch them learn . . .

(Phillipa Rouet, Withywood Community School, Bristol. Taken from Clarke, 2005)

Co-constructing success criteria

Although it might seem quicker and easier to simply give students a list of success criteria linked to a learning intention, there is a tendency then for the criteria to be misunderstood or even ignored. In any case, being given a list of criteria without seeing them applied removes a crucial element of success – being able to see and analyze what a good one or different versions of good ones look like in advance.

The impact of co-constructed success criteria:

- students become more independent,
- students have more ownership over their learning and ongoing evaluation,
- there is higher achievement when students have seen good examples and can follow or choose from the success criteria they have generated,
- older students can teach younger students more effectively,
- higher achievers can teach lower achievers more effectively,
- teachers have greater assurance that the students understand the criteria.

Teachers have evolved several effective strategies for co-constructing success criteria, all of which are an investment in quality. The following examples show how much more is being done than simply gathering success criteria, namely internalizing them in context, identifying them in the first place, seeing what excellence does or does not look like, having a thoughtful dialogue with a learning partner and the teacher about the possible criteria and their meanings.

Strategies used by teachers to co-construct criteria

(Most efficient method is to ask learning partners to have a 30-second discussion to identify one feature each time. The features are then gathered and written up by the teacher as they are generated):

1. **Showing excellent and different examples of the same skill either in written form or finished product and asking, 'What features can you identify in these examples?'**

   This strategy works very well with short extracts of writing, examples of art, design and technology and so on, and analysis of previous examples helps scaffold understanding and develop expertise.

2. **Demonstrating a technique or skill (possibly projected if, for instance, drawing the stages of a line graph) stopping after each step and asking, 'What did I just do?'**

   Demonstrating a particular art technique, for instance, or specific skill, such as looking up words in a dictionary, with the teacher thinking out loud throughout, helps students identify the steps or ingredients of the skill. They can be asked repeatedly, 'What did I just do?' as a way of gathering the criteria. Older students can compile their own success criteria during the demonstration. This technique can also be used to develop quality in writing for instance, where the teacher thinks aloud her choice of words, encouraging students to call out better words or phrases.

3. **Demonstrating good and bad/showing good and bad examples of old student work**

   PE, music and art are examples of subjects for which a practical demonstration of how to do the skill well and how to do it badly both entertained students as well as helping them identify key features. Seeing a good example alongside a poor example helps students identify more clearly what should be included and what should not, or what makes the difference between good and better.

4. **Doing it wrong**

   *The teacher demonstrates how **not** to do the task in hand, inviting students to correct her and draw up the criteria as they go along. Especially good for mathematics with closed elements and very popular with young students.*

5. **Showing a wrong example**

   One teacher showed her class a really bad example of how to film someone. Students offered advice to the film-maker, thus generating the success criteria.

   Another teacher showed a diagrammatic write up of an experiment to see which liquids rot teeth the fastest. None of the variables were constant and students could see what should stay the same and what should change, so were able to generate the criteria for a fair test.

   Showing a calculation from old student work in which there is an error is powerful in forcing students to analyze the mathematics step by step, thus generating the criteria as well as seeing common errors.

6. **Working through it**

   Analysing a bar graph, for instance, and discussing what helped students interpret it, is a good way of pulling out its elements.

7. Retrospective co-construction

Students asked to play a playground game then had to explain how the game was played to their partner. Their discussions were then analyzed as a class (they had used time connectives, ordering steps and so on) and instruction success criteria were generated with examples. In another example, students were given a mathematics problem to solve. After regular intervals they were asked to share strategies, which were written up as the success criteria.

8. Incomplete surprise letter or invitation

By providing a surprise which is incomplete, (such as an invitation with missing information), students instinctively want to include the missing elements which then amount to the success criteria (e.g. Where is the party? What time? Who is it from? etc. – all success criteria for an invitation).

9. Jigsaw the pieces

By cutting up the pieces of, for instance, an excellent newspaper report, persuasive argument, write up of a scientific experiment and inviting students to reassemble them, they are involved in analysis of the content matter. This leads to the generation of the ingredients but also gives an example of what a good one looks like.

10. Reordering given success criteria after practical experience

One teacher of 5-year-olds presented the students with three success criteria cards for a science experiment, which she needed to be put in order. They had previously conducted a simple experiment, made predictions and so on, so the task had the previous experience for them to hook the criteria on.

11. Eavesdropping talk partners *(good when you think students will probably already know something about this, such as the elements involved in working out the meanings of unknown words).*

Asking students to decide the success criteria for a learning intention and simply walking around jotting down their ideas is an efficient way of gathering success criteria.

12. Sloppy success criteria

Especially good for mathematics, a calculation with errors is presented alongside its success criteria. The success criteria have been followed correctly, so what has gone wrong? Students have to analyze the steps, the errors and put right the success criteria.

4. The stages of the SOLO taxonomy

Biggs and Collis (1982) devised the SOLO taxonomy, 'the structure of the observed learning outcome'. SOLO is a means of classifying the learning outcomes in terms of their complexity, enabling us to assess students' learning in terms of its quality rather than how much has been learnt. The basic structure of SOLO is that we start with no idea about any topic, then one idea, then many ideas (surface learning)

What are the five SOLO levels of understanding?

SOLO shows students' learning outcomes at these five levels:

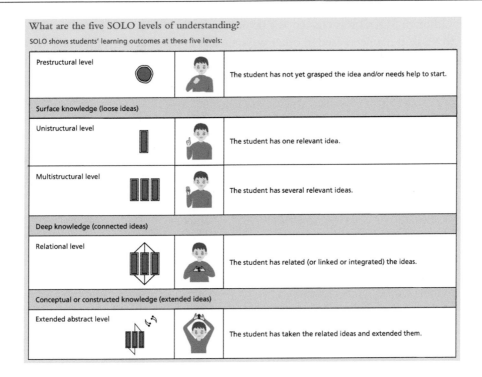

Prestructural level			The student has not yet grasped the idea and/or needs help to start.
Surface knowledge (loose ideas)			
Unistructural level			The student has one relevant idea.
Multistructural level			The student has several relevant ideas.
Deep knowledge (connected ideas)			
Relational level			The student has related (or linked or integrated) the ideas.
Conceptual or constructed knowledge (extended ideas)			
Extended abstract level			The student has taken the related ideas and extended them.

Figure 3.2 The SOLO taxonomy

(www.pamhook.com)

then we make links between and extending the ideas (deep learning) and finally we can transfer, apply and extend our ideas (see Figure 3.2). This is a model of how learning builds up which is especially useful in **assessing, categorizing and planning**. The major reason for including SOLO in this book is that it helps hone the feedback to the level, or just above the level the student is working at; it helps determine the next level of challenge and it can be used to structure appropriate questions or tasks at or just above where the student is in their learning taxonomy. One of its greatest powers is that it can be used to feedforward and feedback.

Of particular use are various versions of the verbs one might attach to the SOLO levels, because they inform the planning and assessment more fully, and have the capacity to give students access to the different stages:

SOLO verbs	
One idea	name, identify, recall, find, label, list
Many ideas	describe, list, classify, continue, complete
Linked ideas	justify, analyze, apply, compare, contrast, relate, explain the cause
Extended ideas	create, generate, hypothesize, design, construct, predict, produce, invent, argue

Although SOLO was created as a taxonomy of the structure of a student's response to a task, it has been used in other ways, such as in the structure of the task itself. The science verbs linked to SOLO (Figure 3.3) from St. Katherine's School, Bournemouth, written by Emma Brookes, were linked with the following plans (Figure 3.4). Their use has led to a clear progression of the development of biology skills:

SOLO taxonomy – science verbs from KS1&2 national curriculum 2013

1. Unistructural	2. Multistructural	3. Relational	4. Extended abstract
• associate • carry out tests • define • identify • know • label diagrams • measure • name • notice • observe • observe changes • perform test • pronounce vocabulary • read vocabulary • recognize • repeat readings • spell vocabulary • test • use equipment • use knowledge • use scientific vocabulary • use symbols	• communicate ideas • construct • control variables • demonstrate • describe • explore • find out • investigate • measure • plan investigations • present data • recognize variables • record data • report findings • research • use keys	• answer questions • ask questions • classify • compare • decide • describe differences/similarities • distinguish • draw simple conclusions • explain • explain degree of trust • find patterns • find relationships • give reasons • group • identify differences and similarities of changes • identify evidence which supports or refutes ideas • interpret • justify • notice patterns • predict without reasons • use evidence to answer questions • use evidence to support findings	• conclude using generalizations • predict giving reasons • predict new values • raise further questions • suggest improvements • use results to make predictions • use results to plan further tests

Figure 3.3 Science verbs linked to SOLO

SOLO taxonomy – examples from KS1&2 biology

	1. Unistructural	2. Multistructural	3. Relational	4. Extended abstract
Y1	Identify/name animals. Define one of: herbivore, omnivore, carnivore, mammal, fish, bird, amphibian or reptile.	Research to find out if animals are herbivores, omnivores, carnivores, mammals, fish, birds, amphibians or reptiles.	Group/classify known animals as herbivores, omnivores, carnivores, mammals, fish, birds, amphibians or reptiles.	Predict how to group unknown animals as herbivores, omnivores, carnivores based on the shape of teeth, etc. Generalize about mammal, fish, bird, amphibian and/or reptile being herbivore, omnivore or carnivore and conclude that there is no connection.
Y2	Define one of: offspring, living, dead, never been alive, diet, habitat, food chain, . . .	Explore the features of things that are living, dead, never been alive. Find out about and describe the basic needs of animals for survival.	Compare the differences between things that are living, dead, never been alive. Classify things as living, dead, never been alive.	Generalize about how to classify things as living, dead, never been alive. Predict with reasons for difficult examples: fire, deciduous tree in winter, seed, etc.
Y3	Define one of: nutrition, diet, protein, carbohydrate, fat, vitamins, canine, incisor, molar, . . .	Research the right types and amount of nutrition for different animals.	Classify different foods as protein, carbohydrate, fat.	Research, plan and evaluate the diet for an athlete, spaceman, different pets, etc.
Y4	Define one of: animal, mammal, fish, bird, amphibian, reptile, vertebrate, invertebrate, producer, consumer, predator, prey.	Use/construct a key or food chain.	Classify animals as vertebrates, invertebrates, mammal, fish, bird, amphibian, reptile, slugs and snails, worms, spiders or insects.	Predict with reasons what would happen to the animals in a food chain if the environment changes and one of the species reduces/dies out.

Figure 3.4 SOLO verbs used for science planning *(continued overleaf)*

	1. Unistructural	2. Multistructural	3. Relational	4. Extended abstract
Y5	Define and identify one of: animal, mammal, fish, bird, amphibian, reptile, vertebrate, invertebrate.	Describe the lifecycles of a mammal, amphibian, insect and bird.	Describe the similarities and differences between the lifecycles of a mammal, amphibian, insect and bird.	Generalize about the lifecycles of a mammal, amphibian, insect and bird.
Y6	Define one of: micro–organism, animal, vertebrate, mammal, fish, bird, amphibian, reptile, invertebrate, porifera, annelids, cnidarians, echinoderms, arthropods, molluscs.	Use and construct classification keys for animals from local habitats based on specific characteristics.	Classify vertebrates, invertebrates and micro-organisms.	Predict with reasons how to classify unfamiliar animals from a broad range of other habitats and research to check.

Figure 3.4 (*Continued*)

SOLO does not work simply as a one-track system. It is possible, for instance, for a long-term learning intention or topic to be spread over days or weeks, with the stages (surface, deep and transfer) as its structure. Within that structure, however, the various elements for individual lessons move from surface to deep, sometimes within the space of a lesson. Similarly, individual students might be at different stages in their learning during that lesson and the whole unit. There is, therefore, a nesting structure for SOLO, with short-term learning taking place within a long-term structure.

In the teaching of writing the focus of the lesson might be a new skill, such as the use of similes. This will be surface knowledge acquired and consolidated, but the process of including these in any writing requires then moving into deep and transferred knowledge. This example could be true for many other subjects, where a new skill is introduced but applied within a bigger context. It is possible, therefore, for all levels to be operating at once for any student, especially where any new skill is being learnt.

How is this useful? We see the surface, deep, transfer stages as helping shape the way in which we see student learning developing, steering us away from focusing on grades or seeing learning as a tick list of knowledge and skills. We also see SOLO as a framework to providing optimal feedback aimed at the level of where the students are currently learning, and importantly, also 'plus one' – feedback aimed to help students move upwards from the learning stage they are at to the next level.

Tracy Jones, the school leader from Merllyn School in Bagillt, created the following SOLO structure to help young students take ownership of their social development (Figure 3.5).

Other examples from the school, used by teachers to plan next steps and inform teaching are shown in the table below:

	Telling people what I need	Learning time	Writing my name
No idea	I need help to say what I need.	I can't do this. I need help.	I can spot my own name, but I need help to write it.
One idea	I can say what I need if someone asks me.	I can do this if someone is beside me and helping me.	I can copy the letters in my name if it is written for me.
Many ideas	I can say what I need.	I can have a try. I am a bit worried I will make mistakes.	I can write some of the letters in my name. They might not be in the right order.
Linked ideas	I can say what I need and explain why I need it.	I can try for myself and I know it's ok to make a mistake – it's how I learn!	I can write my name with all the letters in the right order.
Extended ideas	I can say what I need and explain why I need it and I can listen and respond to others' needs.	I can help someone else learn what I now know.	I can spot the letters from my name as I learn to read and write new words.

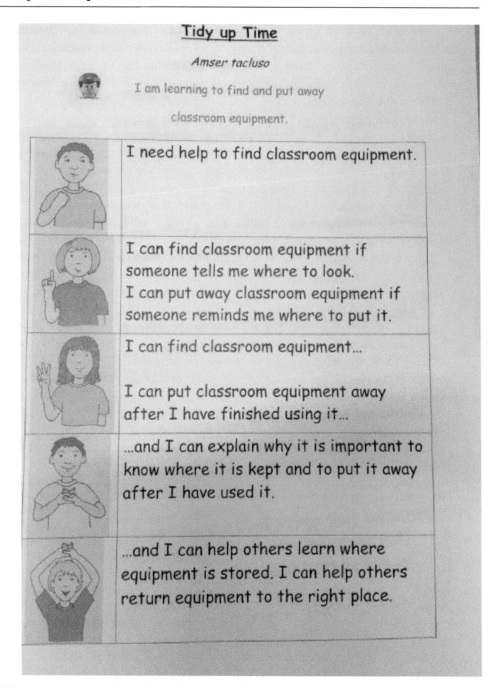

Tidy up Time

Amser tacluso

I am learning to find and put away classroom equipment.

	I need help to find classroom equipment.
	I can find classroom equipment if someone tells me where to look. I can put away classroom equipment if someone reminds me where to put it.
	I can find classroom equipment... I can put classroom equipment away after I have finished using it...
	...and I can explain why it is important to know where it is kept and to put it away after I have used it.
	...and I can help others learn where equipment is stored. I can help others return equipment to the right place.

Figure 3.5 Early years use of SOLO

Finally, an anecdote about the use of SOLO in planning and re-planning according to student feedback from Megan Thomas, Roebuck School in Stevenage:

Anecdote

My Y6 math class (10–11-year-olds) started with 1 idea (what is division – the opposite of multiplication), many ideas (divide by 2, 3, 4, 5, 6, 7, 8 and 9 with numbers up to 4 digits), linked ideas (long division methods – what is the same/what is different), extended ideas (able to divide any number choosing the appropriate method. Students were more secure in the method and understood more deeply. They can now apply more effectively to different situations.

One idea

The students in my class are very wobbly on their methods. We needed to go back to check basic understanding. Asking 'What is division?' helped link their understanding to multiplication and their mathematics facts, showing that division is the inverse. The link with fractions and sharing was also explored. Students realised that knowing tables can help them divide 2 digits by the numbers 1–12 (e.g. 8x7 = 56, 56 divided by 7 = 8, 56 divided by 8 = 7.

Many ideas

Once we got into dividing 3- and 4-digit numbers we realised we could still use multiplication in jottings but needed a more efficient method.
5 divided into 480
How many 5s divide into 4? 0
How many 5s divide into 48? 9 remainder 3
How many 5s divide into 30? 6
Jottings
(5x table)

Linked ideas

Once students were secure with this method (finding remainders expressed as decimals and fractions) I showed them a completed long division and said what is the same/what is different? At first students could identify division as shapes and jottings for the tables. Seeing the subtraction made them link to division being repeated subtraction.

E.g. 25 into 4500 as a long division sum means you keep subtracting

> *The class used 'Does McDonalds Sell Cheese Burgers?' to remember divide, multiply (jottings), subtract, check, bring it down.*
> *The method was practised again with decimals and remainders.*

Extended ideas

Students were now secure with the method and could answer questions with missing numbers (e.g. a long division sum completed but with some missing numbers).

SOLO warning!

As with anything which looks like a linear model of learning, it is easy to fall into a trap of labeling students by the SOLO steps and setting up a new type of ability grouping, where all students working at each stage are sitting together. **This is not wise and not advised.** Students move through the SOLO phases depending more on how you structure the learning in that lesson, and labeling them can condemn them to a level, and ignores the ebb and flow of learning. Learning is more a staccato than a linear process. When the use of surface, deep, transfer is used for planning and observation to guide feedback, on the other hand, we see the greatest benefits. More detail about these stages now follows.

The stages of learning

The main reason that feedback information is so variable in its effectiveness is because the feedback information needs to be aligned to where the student is in the learning cycle, and, if it is not then the feedback is likely to be misinterpreted, misheard or ignored. In brief:

1. *when the student is working at the 'idea' or* **surface knowledge phase***, then feedback directed to the correct or incorrectness of the task is very valuable,*
2. *when the student is working at* **relating or linking ideas***; or,*
3. **extending the ideas***, then feedback directed to the process strategies and self-regulation (making own improvements), and not so much to the task, is very valuable.*

At all times, aim most of the feedback at the current level of learning, but provide 'plus one' feedback with the aim of moving the student to the next level of cognitive complexity.

The following paragraphs describe in detail the three levels of feedback aligned with the stages of learning:

The first level of feedback: surface information

The first level is feedback about the task, usually in terms of specific directions to acquire more, different or correct information. It often requires re-teaching, and the feedback can be more correct or incorrect, acquiring more or different information, and feedback is focused on how well the task is being accomplished or performed. Such feedback usually aims to help acquisition, storing, reproduction and use of knowledge. This level is powerful when learning content, the ideas or surface level knowledge: a prerequisite to the ability to then relate these ideas, seeing links between them. Teaching and learning should focus on learning the correct information so as to later move to relating this information to other ideas.

An example of feedback at the surface or task level:

'*Your learning goal was to structure your recount in a way that the first thing you write is the first thing you did. Then you write about the other things you did in the same order that they happened. The success criteria we created together include that the events must be in the order they happened. Remember the example we went through? You have written the first thing first, but after that it becomes muddled. You need to go through what you have written and number the order in which things happened and re-write them in that order*'.

Too often students see the main game in class is to 'know a lot' – to emulate Siri or Google. Indeed, many of the tasks and tests they are asked to complete reinforce this notion. Focusing on the success criteria of the learning intention help focus students on remembering and understanding processes, and therefore to deeper understanding. We argue that knowing lots can be helpful, provided the lesson moves to relating these single ideas, extending and exploring them then learning to transfer them to other contexts. Surface is a prerequisite to deeper, not an end point.

The second level of feedback: knowing the processes involved in getting the task done

The second level is feedback aimed at the processes used to create the product or complete the task (e.g. success criteria, analysis of good examples and how they were achieved). Such feedback can lead to alternative processing, reduction of cognitive load, can provide strategies for error detection, reassessment of approach, cueing to seek more effective information search and use of task strategies. Feedback at this process level appears to more effective than at the task level for enhancing deeper learning, and there can be a powerful interactive effect between feedback aimed at improving the strategies and processes and feedback aimed at the more surface task information. The latter can assist in improving task confidence and self-efficacy, which in turn provides resources for more effective and innovative information and strategy searching. Chan (2006) induced a failure situation for students, then found that formative rather than summative feedback, and self-referenced rather than any comparison to other students in the class, was more likely to enhance students' self-efficacy.

Two examples of feedback at this process level:

You are stuck on this word (reading to the teacher) and you looked at me instead of trying to work it out yourself. Can you work out why you might have got it wrong and then can you try a different strategy? Like clues in the pictures?

> *You have been asked to compare these ideas – for example you could try to see how they are similar, how they are different and then how they relate together.*

The third level of feedback: students take more control

The third level is more focused at the self-regulation level, and relates to greater skill in self-evaluation, confidence to engage further in the task, further seeking and accepting and accommodating feedback information. This feedback increases the student's capability to create internal feedback and to self-assess, enhances the willingness to invest effort into seeking and dealing with feedback information and leads to internal attributions (I am really getting this) more than external attributions (I got this right because she likes me) about success or failure. At this level, the learner takes more control and there are many direct links to self-as-learner, which includes attributions of self-assessment, self-help seeking, self-appraisal and self-management.

Two examples of feedback at this self-regulation level:

I am impressed by how you went back to the beginning of the sentence when you became stuck on this word. But in this case, it didn't help. What else could you do? When you decide on what the word means, I want to tell you how confident you are and why.

You checked your answer with the resource book (self-help) and found you got it wrong. Any idea as to why you got it wrong? (error detection). What strategy did you use? Can you think of another strategy to try and how else could you work it out if you are correct?

This highest level leads to the development of assessment capable learners who: know where they are going, know what and how to do what they are supposed to be doing in the learning according to the success criteria, have many learning strategies and know how to select the right strategies for the task at hand, strive for challenging tasks (not too hard, not too boring), can monitor their progress, know how to seek and interpret feedback from others (teacher, peers, the resources), know how to think aloud to test ideas with others, see error as opportunities to learn, are able to recognize when they are ready for what's next, know what to do next and enjoy the thrill of this learning (Frey, Hattie & Fisher, 2018).

The practical strategies and processes outlined in this book are strongly linked with these three levels. When students have co-constructed success criteria and analyzed together what makes a good example or what went wrong in a poor example, or one with errors, they are equipped with understanding the steps or ingredients involved in a task, as well as developing a 'nose for quality' and what success might look like. When one student's work is projected mid lesson for all to analyze for successes and 'possible improvements' so far, students are being trained in the processes involved in self-assessment and self-regulation as well as learning from each other's successes and improvement points. When learning powers or dispositions are embedded in learning, discussed and linked with learning intentions and the task in hand, then students have access to strategies for when they are 'stuck' and are encouraged to use the various dispositions (perseverance, peer support and so on) to enhance their learning.

The culture described in **Chapter 1** and the four learning strategies described in this chapter form the framework within which we can give and receive effective feedback. **Prior knowledge, learning intentions, success criteria and the three stages of learning** help give teachers and learners a point of reference, a focus which will steer them in the right direction, leading to appropriate feedback and therefore greater learning. We need to frame the feedback at or just above the level that the student is operating at, and this increases the probability that they will understand it, use it and value feedback.

When we started this book, we noted that feedback is indeed powerful, but also variable in its effectiveness. This chapter has pointed to a way through this variability. That is, it is critical to know the optimal form of feedback to provide the student related to where they are in the learning cycle, what they already know and understand (prior knowledge), how the feedback is connected to the purposes of learning (learning intentions) and reducing the gap between where they are and where they need to be (success criteria).

There is another critical element in this feedback story – not only the providing of feedback but teaching students (and teachers) how to interpret and use the feedback they are given. Hence, the next chapter starts to uncover the evidence about feedback and the kinds of practical strategies used by teachers and students in giving and receiving effective feedback *during lessons*. Clearly the culture and practice outlined in the chapters so far is to be built on in enabling that feedback to be as effective as it can be.

Key points

- Prior knowledge discussion questions give feedback to teachers which confirm or disconfirm plans for that lesson, thus allowing adjustment.

- Learning intentions must be known to students, but not necessarily at the start of a lesson. They should be authentic, clear and decontextualized, so that skills can be transferred to other contexts and subjects.
- Success criteria need to be co-constructed to maximize their impact. They are either compulsory elements in the case of closed learning intentions (rules) or choice items when linked with open learning intentions (tools).
- The SOLO taxonomy (surface, deep, transfer) is useful for understanding students' developing thinking, helping to move +1 up the taxonomy and for planning, assessment and providing appropriate feedback.

4

The power of in-lesson verbal feedback

So far we have established a culture within which feedback is most effective, and described learning frameworks which give purpose and meaning to the feedback given or received.

This chapter unravels the many interwoven, mostly verbal feedback exchanges which take place, in the moment, during lessons. We begin by looking at the most significant research findings about feedback as it relates to the classroom experience, then focus on student to teacher feedback before teacher to student and students to each other.

Why within the lesson and verbal is best

Our starting point is the importance of feedback happening, where possible, during the learning rather than after. There are many possible analogies which make this blindingly obvious, especially in the context of physical activity. Imagine a coach writing down his tips to the football team rather than talking and listening to the players during the half time break.

A teacher of 11-year-olds sent the following email to us:

> I had a real moment of clarity about instant feedback whilst I was on a residential trip with my class. They were abseiling and I was watching and listening to how the leaders were teaching them to abseil. The feedback was immediate and the children responded to it: 'straighten your back; move your feet further apart; feed the rope through'. I suddenly realised how pointless this feedback would have been walking back to the minibus or back at the centre – a missed opportunity.
>
> *(Rachael Clargo Winchcombe, Abbey School)*

Now imagine a student writing a characterization, handing it in, then getting it back with an improvement suggestion a few days later – compared to a lesson in which half way through the writing, one student's work is projected for a class analysis of its successes so far and suggestions for improvements. Analysing their own attempts, the class resumes writing, constantly self reviewing for successes and improvement possibilities. Paired collaborative discussion follows, focusing on one person's writing at a time, in which, again, successes are pointed out with reasons given and improvement suggestions are offered.

This scenario will be described in more detail during this chapter, but for now serves to illustrate the potential and power of verbal feedback taking place in 'the golden moment' when the context is alive, the student is 'in flow' and the learning is gaining momentum.

1. Feedback links

In gauging how and when to give feedback, how often and how much, it is useful to see the results of various key studies around the theme of feedback. Student self-efficacy and their trust in the teacher and fellow students is a vital starting point, but our knowledge of how we remember or forget things also helps us in the complex process of determining appropriate feedback. The impact of positive and negative feedback is also explored and distinguishing between feedback as given and feedback as received is, of course, the crux of the matter if we are to impact student learning at all.

Student self-efficacy

Self-efficacy is the term which describes the level of confidence we have in ourselves to reach our goals. This should not be confused with self-esteem, which is how we feel about ourselves as individuals, and has much less impact on our achievements at school. I might decide that I am a nice person (high self-esteem) but no good at school (low self-efficacy) or think I am a high achiever (high self-efficacy) but believe that nobody likes me (low self-esteem). Before we begin to understand student understanding and how to respond to what we think we see, we need to be sensitive to how student self-efficacy affects students' answers to our questions, to their motivation and their effort.

High self-efficacy

High self-efficacious students are more likely to make more optimistic predictions about their performance after initial failure than after initial success. Such failure could be because of criticism, pointing out of errors or insufficient quality, or some form of disconfirmation of how well the student thought of his or her work. These students feel highly able, so negative feedback simply spurs them on and they are likely to even seek it, because they know it will extend their skill level (Bandura, 1997).

Low self-efficacy

Students with low self-efficacy can react negatively to both positive and negative feedback but respond positively to ability feedback ('You are mastering these problems') and effort ('You've been working really hard'). Care is needed, however, as positive feedback about initial success ('Great start – you got the tens column right!') might be interpreted as confirmation that they had a deficiency that needed to be remedied. They might engage to further deepen the skill in question but, in the long term, these students can avoid investing effort in learning if they are told they are making errors or if further tests disconfirm their efforts. Disconfirming feedback is likely to have the greatest negative impact on subsequent motivation for low efficacious students – they are likely to experience negative emotions, show less motivation for a subsequent task and attribute the feedback less to effort and more to their perceived ability (Hattie & Timperley, 2007).

Carol Dweck's work on student's reactions to feedback (2000) revealed that students with low self-efficacy more typically attribute success or failure as follows (ideal scenarios italicized and in red):

	Success	Failure
Internal factor	I did well at this test	I didn't do well at this test
External factor	I did well because the teacher likes me	I didn't do well because the teacher doesn't like me
Stable	I'm good at this subject	I'm no good at this subject
Unstable	I was lucky	I was unlucky
Specific	I'm good at this subject but who knows about the others	I'm no good at this subject but who knows about the others
Global	I'm good at this so I'll be good at everything	I'm no good at this so I'll be no good at anything

Kluger and DeNisi (1996) found that when students are given feedback, they can do one of four things: change behavior, change the goal, abandon the goal or reject the feedback. Clearly we want students to change their behaviors (unless they have achieved the goal, in which case we want them to aspire to a higher goal), particularly by increasing their effort and aspirations rather than ignore the feedback or decide the work is too easy (at least they can find a higher challenge) or too hard (likely to give up).

Underpinning much of this is the level of trust generated between teachers and students. Students need the knowledge that the teacher cares about and likes them, that they are safe, that peers will not disparage them, that they will not lose face if they ask a question and will be treated with respect. They can then make their learning visible: question, ask for help or share misconceptions. Without this they are already on the back foot when given feedback. Their lack of trust means their engagement with the feedback will be limited, they might choose not to 'hear' or interpret the feedback, and their motivation to act upon it led mainly by compliance.

Remembering and forgetting

As so much of our job is helping students to be able to remember a great deal of what they are taught, including any feedback they might receive, it is useful to know what research tells us about memory. Remembering consists of acquiring memories (encoding), putting them somewhere (storage) and finding them when we want them (retrieval). Our working memory is simply, in the present moment, a) what we are paying attention to and b) the ongoing retrieval of related memories which help us makes sense of what we are learning. As humans, our working memory capacity can be quite limited.

Cognitive Load Theory

When our working memory is overloaded, learning is minimal, so knowing how to maximize cognitive load has clear implications for teaching.

Cognitive Load Theory was developed by John Sweller in 1988 (Figure 4.1). The widely accepted model of CLT is that the process of human information processing has three parts: sensory memory, working memory and long-term memory. Information from our sensory memory (everything we see, hear and feel) passes through our working memories and is then mostly discarded, focusing on only what matters at the time (*e.g. at this moment I can hear birds singing, a gardener in*

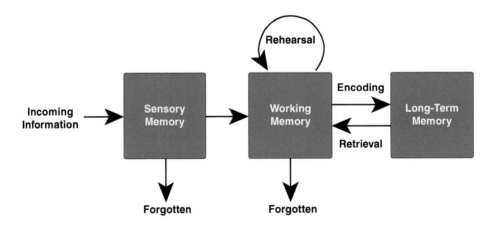

Figure 4.1 Cognitive Load Theory

(Adapted from Atkinson, R.C. and Shiffrin, R.M. (1968), 'Human memory: a proposed system and its control processes' in Spence. K.W. and Spence, J.T. (Eds.), *The Psychology of Learning and Motivation*, (vol.2) New York: Academic Press pp. 89–95) *someone's garden, a door closing, my husband typing and a car in the distance, but I am writing these sentences so everything else is discarded while I focus on how to best explain cognitive load theory!).*

We can hold between five and nine items (or chunks) of information at any one time. It is very difficult to hold eleven random numbers, for instance, in our working memories. Try 84739013421! If we can chunk any of them into single items, the possibilities become greater (e.g. the code for my town is 01342, which is stored in my long-term memory, which counts as one item in this string of numbers for me, so I now have only the other five numbers to memorize.)

When we process information, we need to learn how to categorize it, then move it into long-term memory *(e.g. dog, cat, animal, buying something in a shop, catching a ball).*

Implications for teaching

- Since working memory has a limited capacity, we should avoid overloading students with additional activities that don't directly contribute to learning. For example, compare Figure 4.1 with Figure 4.2, where the diagram is now represented with the labels listed at the side, which places greater demand on our working memory because our attention is 'split' as we look back and forth between the information.

- When presenting students with information, we need to incorporate visual and written cues as far as possible so that working memory can deal with it more easily. Visual and auditory channels should be combined where possible to extend working memory (e.g. a video clip with narration rather than additional screen text: Mayer & Moreno, 1998). Watching a PowerPoint, for example, while also paying attention to the speaker talking about it can be manageable and useful for most people, but can be hard for some of us (Horvath, 2014).

- Break learning into parts which can be linked. The more connections, forming chunks, the less our working memory is overloaded. Linking items is the beginning of deep understanding.

- Analyzing examples of excellence as a class eases the cognitive load, as the student sees not only how the learning in question has been applied, but also what good learning looks like. The alternative would be to present bits of information then ask the students to do the work: no connections and no way of chunking, and then the cognitive load is heavier. *As a student (SC) in school in the 60s and 70s, history was 'taught' in my school as a set of dates and single liners (e.g. 1066 Battle of Hastings) which we had to copy into our books. A whole exercise book of these had to be learnt for the end of year test. I tried to memorize them but only managed to remember 3 or 4 pages. Looking back, I can see that, had these sets of dates been chunked (e.g. between 1000 and 1066) with linking stories about the historical events, I would have more easily been able to learn and memorize each chunk.* If we can show students how many ostensibly separate items link and make memorable chunks (e.g. all the ways in which Pythagoras' Theorem occur in the syllabus).

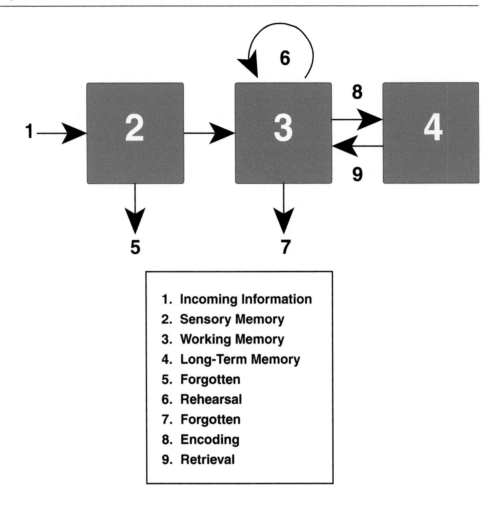

Figure 4.2 Cognitive Load Theory 2

(Taken from 'Cognitive Load Theory – helping people learn effectively' in www.mindtools.com)

we can help to ease the cognitive load. We need both the surface knowledge and the relationships between them to effect learning.

Desirable difficulties and memory

Robert Bjork (1994a) and Bjork and Kroll (2015) expounded the theory of 'desirable difficulties' – that by making information more difficult to encode we can improve our ability to retrieve it later. So by making students 'think hard' about subject content (seeking challenge as the essence of the growth mindset), the more likely they are to remember it. We should also not give too much help or feedback which takes away the cognitive demand of the task. It is common in mathematics lessons, for instance, for struggling students to have the steps broken down when solving a problem to such an extent that the task is emptied of the mathematical 'big ideas' (Brousseau, 1997). Better, perhaps, to ask questions about the student's efforts so far which give them a way forward without telling them precisely what to do at every step. When breaking down into smaller, easier steps a piano piece, a gymnastics move, the conventions of grammar or a specific mathematical algorithm, we still need to keep the challenge factor alive as well as rooting the small step clearly within the big picture of the whole task.

Forgetting helps us remember

Bjork's work on memory (2011), has shown us that forgetting is also an important stage of learning, because when we encounter the learning again we are more likely to remember and store it in our long-term memory: *'Forgetting, rather than undoing learning, creates the opportunity to reach additional levels of learning'*. We might have forgotten or not be able to retrieve vocabulary in a language we haven't used for years, for instance, but the words are stored and, as we revisit the vocabulary, we find that the act of remembering is much faster than it was the first time around. We appear to also have greater capacity to learn more vocabulary. Perhaps we need to think about things students have forgotten in the same way we think about error and misconceptions: they are evidence, perhaps, of being on the brink of stronger and deeper learning when concepts or skills are retaught. We are not giving feedback which 'starts again', but instead rebuilding, with the student's stronger glue, forgotten ideas – now easier to relearn.

The link with spaced or distributed practice

What we know about forgotten learning is one of the reasons underpinning the finding that *practice spaced out over time* in short sessions is much more successful for learning than *massed practice all at one time*. Having multiple opportunities over time to learn, and being given feedback about our understanding over time, is more likely to cause connections between ideas and stronger associations with what we already know, thus we are more likely to retain the learning in long-term memory.

Distributed practice and interleaved practice

Bjork's research (1994b) suggests that interleaving the spaced practice helps long-term memory, so that the various skills and knowledge are dipped into frequently, and sometimes in different settings, so that students become used to accessing the relevant information more easily in any situation. It seems that frequent quiz or classroom tests of everything learnt so far is essential in keeping the retrieval mechanisms working, with items mixed (e.g. a mathematics test including all skills covered this year, rather than one area of study).

Context and memory

How students remember things depends on a number of factors, one of which is the context in which it was placed. Meaningful contexts have been an ideal for teachers for decades because we believe that the more we can link concepts or knowledge to real situations, the more likely they are to be understood and remembered. One teacher of 9-year-olds covered map reading skills every year, studying maps then getting the students to find their way around the playground using different maps made by the teacher to a place where they would find 'treasure'. As part of a learning team of teachers experimenting with formative assessment strategies, she involved the students, for the first time, in planning the activities to fulfil the learning intentions she had presented to them for a unit on map reading. The students suggested that they should be given maps to find their way around the town, something the teacher reported she would never have considered, but found a way to make it happen, putting the students in groups with volunteer parents. All started off in the local park and went in different directions following their maps, to the local cinema, in which they all watched a film together. The students did not know the intricacies of the town and were only allowed to use their maps to find their way, so meaning and purpose were combined. Their motivation was enhanced, according to the teacher, by the fact that this was *their idea and they were the 'teachers' of their own learning.*

The teacher, at a feedback session with the team of teachers, said that this event, and the associated map reading skills, were remembered by the students months later. Context matters, although we need to make sure that what students store in their long-term memories is the learning as the lasting memory!

Such real life contexts are hardly possible for every lesson in a school day, but meaningful, real life contexts are possible with some planning. In a lesson (see more detail in Chapter 2) in which school weights were wrapped up, estimated then revealed to 7- and 8-year-olds, a reality check was given when the teacher simply put up a photo of a polar bear and told the class that it weighed one ton, a weight many had guessed their kilogram weight weighed! A photo of an elephant followed (7–10 tons), then a bag of sugar (1kg), then a credit card (5g). Thus, context, purpose and meaning come together with what might have been a set of meaningless measures.

When to give less feedback

We also know that too much feedback too often and too soon before students have time to follow 'stuck strategies' can turn students into feedback junkies, too reliant on advice and therefore less likely to do well when left to their own devices. Judicious withholding, delaying and reducing feedback can boost long-term retention and lead to more sustained learning (Soderstrom & Bjork, 2015). This 'holding back' is more effective after the students have gained the ideas or information (the surface phase) and are moving into relating and extending ideas (the deeper phase). It is the optimal time to encourage the students to follow 'what to do when you are stuck strategies', go into the pit of unknowing (Nottingham, 2017) and let them wallow in error. At the right time after this learning pit, it might be necessary to provide a shower of clean new learning and check the students' understanding and provide appropriate 'where to next' or 'how to improve' feedback.

When to delay feedback

Delaying feedback can have great benefits as it functions as a form of restudy when retrieval strength is low. When *higher achievers*, for instance, provide correct responses, delaying feedback can sometimes increase its strength (they won't see the work as over and might be motivated to check their answers for accuracy). *For lower achievers* it pays to provide immediate feedback, as the cognitive demands can be too high if the feedback is delayed (Li, Zhu & Ellis, 2016). Trying to remember the context, the problems and the processes involved at a later time creates unnecessary difficulties, so immediate feedback is more appropriate.

When feedback follows too quickly after or during learning, and this feedback is either not understood or not enacted by the student, this can reinforce errors, as students associate whatever they did with the feedback they were given, even though they did not hear the feedback! When students see mistakes as in important part of the learning process, they are more likely to hear and value the feedback.

Giving is not receiving

Teachers might claim that they give a great deal of feedback, but the more appropriate measure is to determine what kind of feedback is actually received (and this is not very much). Most teacher feedback is presented to groups or the whole class, which encourages students to often believe that the feedback is not about them – hence the dissipation of well-meaning feedback. Carless (2006) has also shown that teachers consider their feedback far more valuable than the students receiving it. Students unfortunately often find feedback confusing and un-reasoned. Sometimes they think they have understood the teacher's feedback when they have not, and even when they do understand it, they might not know how to use it (Goldstein, 2006). Higgins et al. (2002) argues that:

> Many students are simply unable to understand feedback comments and interpret them correctly.

Much depends on students' understanding of the meaning and nature of feedback; whether the feedback provider is perceived as powerful, fair and trustworthy; and the emotions (rejection or acceptance) associated with the context, level of investment and manner of the delivery of the feedback (kind, helpful, specific compared to hurried, impatient and too general perhaps?). The message is always to check to understand how students interpret the feedback that is provided: 'What did you understand from what I just said? How would you use this feedback in your next learning step? Is there more you want from me right now to help in your learning?'

2. From student to teacher

What matters

The feedback teachers receive *from* students is our first and most important focus. The teaching/learning dynamic becomes synthesized when students are able to communicate their needs to teachers, and when teachers takes account of everything in front of them which constitutes feedback from the student: body language, behaviour, motivation, apparent understanding, misconceptions, avoidance tactics, strategies used and so on. It is hard to accept that sometimes misconceptions or bad behaviour are the result of mismatched tasks to student competence or tasks which are too boring, not sufficiently challenging or unclear, rather than the fault of the student for not being diligent or for being a low achiever, but these are possibilities which must be acknowledged if we are to maximize student achievement.

Look at the responses from a 6-year-old student, from Ross Elementary School, California when questioned by her father, Michael McDowell, about learning and feedback. It would be interesting to know whether the class teacher was aware of her thoughts:

Q: What makes a great learner?

A: Someone who takes feedback and puts it where the teacher says. If you don't know a book you should read slowly. Sometimes before I raise my hand I check my work then I can give myself feedback and fix things. Sometimes I don't like feedback from other people.

Q: How do you feel when you get feedback?

A: I sometimes feel uncomfortable and sometimes OK with it. Sometimes I think I don't want that feedback.

Q: What happens to your brain when you make a mistake?

A: It grows.

Q: When is the best time to have a growth mindset?

A: What I usually do when I make a mistake I don't say 'Oh no!', I say 'Yay! My brain is growing!'

Effective feedback consists of three teacher components as seen below. This forms a continuous cycle of finding out and subsequent feedback, most effectively during lessons, but includes findings from post-lesson information (see next chapter). These three components align with a) Where am I going? b) How am I going? and c) Where to next? How can it be improved?

Teacher	Student
a) *checking to see if the students understand the nature of the learning task and are able to evaluate whether the learning they are doing is good enough,*	Where am I going?
b) *a constant quest to understand students' understanding, rather than to assume, then to*	How am I going?
c) *facilitate appropriate feedback as a result of those findings.*	Where to next? How can it be improved?

These three stages make the process of finding out and giving feedback sound deceptively easy, but, because learning is neither linear nor perceptible (only performance can be seen, although encouraging students to think aloud helps them and their teachers know where they are in the learning cycle) and progresses at different rates with inevitable times of forgetting, it is anything but. Students are unique individuals with different levels of self-efficacy, so we are constantly balancing students' individual needs with the needs of the task; a remarkable achievement considering the number of students in the average class. Current performance can be a highly unreliable guide as to whether learning (i.e. long-term retention and transfer of skills and knowledge) has happened. When we are eliciting current understanding, the first thing to accept is that we cannot ever actually get inside the student's brain and see what they understand. We can only approximate by what we see and hear as a result of our questioning ('What could you do first?' rather than 'So first you have to …') and the expectations of the task. A question like 'How many different ways can you draw shapes with an area of 24 sq.cm?' will reveal more of the student's thinking and understanding than 'Find the area of a rectangle measuring 8cm by 3cm'.

We do the best we can, gradually building up skills and competences, evaluating frequently and spacing the learning rather than teaching 'massed' blocks which get forgotten more easily than if the skills are frequently revisited.

The following sections describe ways in which teachers have used effective strategies to find out what students are thinking and what they do or don't know during the course of a lesson, bearing in mind that we suggested that lessons begin with some kind of discussion probe at prior knowledge before proceeding (see previous chapter). Some of the strategies here are simply gathering techniques (such as eavesdropping) whereas others involve both receiving and then giving feedback in the moment, as well as the feedback being acted upon (as in mid lesson learning stops).

Strategies for uncovering student understanding

Questioning by teachers

Asking good questions of the whole class and then of individuals while they are working, during continual 'walkabouts', is the teacher's main aid to establishing current knowledge or the depth of student understanding while it is happening. Once students are engaged in some independent work, questions can be asked **of individuals** such as these:

- Tell me/show me what you have learnt so far
- Tell me what you're going to do first
- What do you mean by? (key question, even if the teacher thinks s/he knows what they mean by it)
- Why do you think...?
- Give me an example of what you mean (key question as often reveals misconceptions)
- Can you develop on that? Tell me more...
- So why is this one better than that? (key question if concrete example available)
- How could you change this to make it clearer?

The more you probe, the more is revealed, so *'What do you mean by...?'* is a simple way of getting to the heart of student understanding. Such questions should aim to elicit a longer reply by the student than the length of the teacher's question. Many answers given by students are correct but don't reveal the level of their understanding. For example, the answer 'connectives' or 'numerator' might be right, often picked up by knowing it's the right word to say, but *'What do you mean by a connective/cosine?'* or *'Give me an example'* as a follow up to either answer will reveal the student's current understanding. If this is a constant feature of a lesson, all students, over time, will get a good deal of face to face informative questioning by the teacher and lessons will be more effectively redirected as students' understanding is continually revealed. *'So why is this one better than the other one?'*, used when students have examples of good and not so good in front of them, helps focus them by referring to concrete examples. A student struggling to explain how one of the two given balanced arguments could be improved, for instance, can be directed to a specific comparison of say, the use of percentage to back up claims in each, where the improvement need is now more obvious.

These enquiring questions by teachers to seek feedback about their students' understanding can be powerful. Much more so than the typical 'What am I thinking?', 'Who knows the answer to this factual question?' and other typical questions that are common in many classrooms. We know that many teachers ask 150+ of these knowledge questions a day with 90% mainly about the facts and less than 3 seconds' response time needed. There is very little feedback to teachers because of asking this kind of question, except to confirm that the one student who was asked to respond to the question either knows the answer or doesn't. Instead, what is needed are questions, such as the above, which assist us in evaluating their impact, and give guidance for where to go next in the learning.

With random talk partners, 30 seconds, say, can be given for students to discuss any questions directed to the whole class, and some form of randomizer is used to determine who answers, the damaging 'hands up' culture is removed. Thus 'wait time' is extended to include articulation of the thinking.

Questioning by students

To be an independent learner one has to be able to ask questions and continue to ask questions in the quest for new learning and understanding. By equipping students with question stems they can ask each other or teachers, we are not only gathering key information about their current understanding but encouraging independent and deeper thinking. Marty Nystrand (2006) found that the most powerful student questions were **'impact questions'**. By this he meant

a) *questions where what counts as an acceptable answer is not pre-specified (e.g. What do you think would happen if…),*
b) *uptake questions, where the teacher incorporates students' responses into subsequent questions (e.g. So, taking Mia's point, does this change anything?) and,*
c) *the extent to which the teacher allows a student response to modify the topic of discourse (e.g. We agree with Finn that we should also think about…).*

In each case the student is given the opportunity to express what they do and do not know, and allows the teacher to hear the current level of knowing and understanding by the student.

Will Ord, an expert in 'Philosophy for Students', suggests the following questions for teachers and students alike, following a surface to deep journey:

Clarification (surface)	Reason and evidence (surface consolidation)	Implications and consequence (deep)	Explore alternative views (deep consolidation)
Can you explain that?	Why do you think that?	What would be the consequence of that?	Can you put it another way…?
What do you mean by…?	How do we know that?	How would you test to see if that is true?	Is there another point of view…?
Can you give me an example of…?	What are your reasons for…?	What follows (what can we work out) from what you say?	What if someone suggested that…?
How does that help…?	Do you have evidence of…?	Does that view agree with what was said earlier?	What is the difference between that view and…?
Does anyone have a question to ask about that idea?	Can you justify your opinion?		What would someone who disagreed with you say?

(Will Ord, from 'Thinking Education Limited' www.thinkingeducation.co.uk)

Eavesdropping

Talk/learning partners can make students' thinking more transparent as they are given many opportunities to articulate their thinking. Partner discussions, after good teacher questions, present golden opportunities for the teacher to listen in on those often-illuminating conversations before asking random students to share their thoughts with the class. Misconceptions noted lead to 'on the hoof' changes to the lesson. Without this opportunity to hear what students are thinking we might carry on the lesson with misconception being built upon misconception.

Avoiding assumptions

Because of teachers' impossible task of being able to watch every student for every minute of a lesson, inaccurate assumptions are often made when 'visiting' students during a lesson, especially with young or with struggling students, because they rarely speak up to correct a teacher's wrong assumption. The dilemma is that to keep some sort of order in our classrooms, students are taught from an early age to listen, pay attention and not to interrupt the teacher – great for order but not for honest student feedback. To allow for more impact questions and for students to indicate they may not know or understand, it is first necessary to build trust, not only between the teacher and students, but also among the students. Errors thrive in a trusting environment and are stultified in a non-trusting environment. Video evidence captured for Clarke's video platform revealed two examples of inaccurate teacher assumptions:

Example 1

The class of 7-year-olds is asked to show 37 on a place value mat using 10 sticks and ones. We see Student A immediately placing 3 tens in the right place, then counting his ones but stopping as he runs out of units. There are not enough ones on the table for all the students. His neighbour, Student B, also runs out of ones and asks if he can borrow one of Student A's. The first student has by now become bored, has picked up all his ten sticks and happily hands over a unit to his friend. At this point the teacher arrives, sees the first student's empty mat and begins to carefully explain to him how to lay out 37…

Example 2

The class of 6-year-olds is working on 'student initiated mathematics'. One student has chosen to write out her $\times$ 9 table. As she writes, she counts on 9 on her fingers each time. She writes $1 \times 9 = 9, 2 \times 9 = 18, 3 \times 9 = 26, 4 \times 9 = 35$ etc., with all now wrong from 3×9 onwards. The teacher talks to her about how she could check 3 × 9 and they agree she will get paper plates and counters to share out. The camera follows the student for the next few minutes and we see her using one of the plates to pile up some counters and then laying out the other 3 plates to do her sharing. When the teacher arrives she sees 4 plates, all with counters on them and assumes the student is working out 4 × 9 instead of the agreed 3 × 9. She sweeps all the plates away and gets the student to start again.

In neither instance, do we see the student explaining to the teacher what has happened. Instead we see teachers making assumptions by what they see in front of them. Why doesn't the first student say 'We ran out of counters. I know how to set out 37'. Why doesn't the second student say, 'I was using this plate to carry the counters?' If the camera could capture so much just following one student each time, how many more times are similar things happening? As it is impossible to be everywhere at once, it seems that there are two possible solutions: firstly, that students need to be shown, modeled perhaps, how they are given permission to tell the teacher when they have misread a situation; secondly teachers can pre-empt this scenario by first asking 'Can you tell me what you've done so far?' The main message is 'do not presume': seek the feedback from the student about what they think is going on. If one of our prime aims is to get feedback from students and therefore learn more about their current understanding, we need to encourage perhaps bolder responses from them so that they are more accurately represented.

3. From teacher to student and students to each other

Royce Sadler (1989), in his 'closing the gap' construction, states that the first stage of feedback is to possess a concept of the goal or learning intention, discussed in the previous chapter, which also looked at success criteria and analysis of worked examples. The next stages are as follows:

To compare the actual level of performance with the goal

To engage in some appropriate action which leads to some closure of the gap.

Taking this to mean not just at the end of the activity, but during, we see this manifested, in a classroom setting, as students articulating to their peers, and to the teacher, their understanding of the task and how it relates to the success criteria so far. This can be taken further and formalized, so that all are included, during mid lesson learning stops. Commonly, a random student's work, still in progress, is projected, analyzed and discussed by the class with feedback given about successes and possible improvements. Students then give feedback to each other based on the whole class modeling and analysis.

Establishing learning intentions and success criteria gives the framework within which teachers look for current understanding or misconceptions, although, as pointed out in the previous chapter, this does not mean that demonstrated excellence unrelated to the learning intention or success criteria should be ignored. Feedback thrives when the students are aware and have co-constructed the criteria of success and can then see how they are going and what to do next to move towards success.

At the self-regulation level (student able to self-assess, stay focused and so on), the commitment to goals is a major mediator of the effectiveness of positive and negative feedback. Van-Dijk and Kluger (2000) demonstrated that positive feedback increases motivation relative to negative feedback for a task that students '*want to do*' and decreases motivation relative to negative feedback for a task that students '*have to do*'. Thus, when we are committed to a goal we are more likely to learn because of positive feedback, but when we undertake a task that we are not committed to (and hence 'have to do'), we are more likely to learn through negative feedback. We need to be driven, as we used to say. When students are committed to the goals, feedback can trigger

> an internal comparison process, which determines how individuals react to feedback. Upon receiving negative feedback, individuals become more dissatisfied with their previous performance, set higher performance goals for the future, and perform at a higher level than those who receive positive feedback or no feedback at all.
>
> *(Podsakoff & Farh, 1989)*

Positive feedback can enhance both free-choice behaviour (i.e. when students could return to or persist in the activity) and self-reported interest in the activity (Deci, Koestner & Ryan, 1999)

Feedback in the moment

This section describes possible practical scenarios for peer coaching, then moves on to mid lesson feedback stops, specific improvements and collaborative peer marking.

Although teachers move around classrooms continually asking questions or giving feedback when they are not explaining from the front, the last twenty years have been the subject of finding more efficient ways to ensure all students get feedback, from the teacher, and their peers, while they are in the process of learning. The very essence of formative assessment or feedback is the ability to react to the learning during the learning so that it can be enhanced before it is too late. We need to help students to seek, receive and use feedback, teaching them to check their efforts against success criteria and consider exemplars analyzed at the beginning of lessons or during mid lesson learning stops. Feedback happens in all directions and students are activated as learning resources for one another.

Peer feedback

Students need to know that they can seek help from other students, but we need to teach them how to engage in peer cooperation and collaboration in the most effective way.

An unsupported environment often leads to students seeking and gaining incorrect help, which they might not realize is incorrect. Ryan and Shim (2012) distinguished between: a) adaptive help seeking (*asking for help with the learning, such as an explanation or an example*) and b) expedient help seeking (*asking for help which gets the task done, usually the answer*). As students encounter the fast pace of secondary education and early adolescence, expedient help seeking increases. If we are to create independent problem solvers, time invested in discussing and modeling the essential feedback component of adaptive help seeking, is more than worthwhile.

Nuthall (2007), as a result of his extensive exploration of students' private classroom conversations, concluded that students live in three different, interacting worlds when they are at school:

- **The public world**: this is what the teacher sees and manages. Students mostly follow the rules and customs of the classroom, structured by the learning activities and routines.
- **The semi-private world**: ongoing peer relationships. This is the world in which students establish and maintain their social roles and status. Transgressing peer customs can have worse consequences for a student than transgressing classroom rules. This is the world in which adults are usually unaware of clique formation, teasing and bullying.
- **The private world of the child's own mind**: knowledge and beliefs change and grow; individual thinking and learning takes place and home and school spill over into each other.

The significance of these worlds links with the effectiveness of feedback. Our awareness of these findings can increase our sensitivity to when, where and how we give feedback. In the case of peer feedback, Nuthall found that students' conversations within the classroom were often about completion of the task (*'How many have you done?'*) and, if at the surface stage of learning, often contained misleading or incorrect feedback.

The optimal time for peer feedback is after the students have the ideas (the first two stages of SOLO) such that they are ready to make connections and relations between ideas. When still learning the foundations, it can often be more effective to re-teach the concepts than engage in peer feedback. There is little value of other students reinforcing wrong ideas and concepts. But when asking the students to play with ideas, explore relations between ideas and extend their thinking, peer feedback can be most powerful.

When students are consolidating deep learning, the power of working with others is most apparent. This involves skills in seeking help from others, listening to others in discussion and developing strategies to 'speak' the language of learning. It is through such listening and speaking about their learning that students and teachers realise what they do deeply know, what they do not know and where they are struggling to find relationships and extensions. An important strategy is when students become teachers of others and learn from peers, as this involves high levels of regulation, monitoring, anticipation and listening to their impact on the learner.

(Hattie & Donoghue, 2016)

One way to enhance peer feedback is via peer coaching. Slavin, Hurley and Chamberlain (2003) outlined four mechanisms of cooperative learning which maximize feedback among students:

Motivation: students help their peers because it is in their own interests to do so if the rules and expectations for cooperation are well structured, leading to greater effort.

Social cohesion: students help each other because they care about their pairing or group, hence more effort.

Personalization: higher achieving students help lower achieving students and vice versa.

Cognitive elaboration: explanation forces students to think more clearly and consolidate their own understanding.

An example of the development of peer coaching in one school follows, building on these ideas.

Peer coaching in Langford School, Fulham

The idea of peer coaching was first launched in the school with input and video about basketball coaching followed by much discussion and the co-construction of success criteria for the elements of good coaching, as follows:

What makes a good learning coach?
- They help you reflect against the success criteria.
- They don't tell you the answer. Instead they ask questions and make you think.
- They suggest strategies, (e.g. word choice), help you focus on particular elements of the success criteria to improve your learning.
- They are specific, helpful and kind.

The students were then given examples of peer coaching across the subjects, with lots of modeling around projected examples.

Peer coaching was then introduced in mathematics lessons with a further co-construction of what the success criteria would look like for a good mathematics coach, then the same for English lessons. These were the result of modeling and learning stops:

Prompts for being a good learning coach in English

- Is there anything you feel you need help with?
- What impact on the reader do you want to achieve?
- Do you think you are achieving this?
- How successful do you think you have you been against the success criteria?
- How can you include this aspect of the success criteria?
- You could use a simile/metaphor etc. here. Can we think of one?
- Can you think of a better word instead of _____?
- Could you think of any adverbs to put before any verbs in your writing?
- Could you ask the reader a question in your writing?

Prompts for being a good learning coach in mathematics

- Have you followed the success criteria?
- Can you demonstrate that this is the right answer? Explain how you know.
- Would a whiteboard help you?
- Could you draw a diagram?
- What is the rule for (e.g. rounding numbers)?
- How do you know this number is (e.g. divisible by 2/prime/a factor of 32)?
- Let's talk through an example and go through the steps.
- Ask me questions and interrupt me if you don't understand.
- Now can you do this example on your own? Talk me through it.

Student know that they have to ask questions first in the coaching process and, if their partner can't get to the answer on their own, they need to explain, or work together to seek the answers.

Student are encouraged to use whiteboards and diagrams on paper to help their explanations and in their working out.

Every week they have a new random partner who they work with, peer coaching each other. Sometimes someone will say *'I really understand this so I can explain it to someone else'*.

Peer coaching in the school is now linked with the three learning zones (*see Chapter 2: panic zone, learning zone, comfort zone*). Students coach each other when marking home learning activities and in mathematics lessons and are very keen to help their learning partners or others in the class. The quality is regulated by regular 'what went well/what didn't go well' discussions after lessons in which coaching has figured.

Students' and teacher's comments about peer coaching in mathematics lessons with random partners in Langford School

10/11-year-olds

Coaching is when a fellow student asks you questions to help you understand a question you are confused about. These questions should eventually lead you to the answer of the question. What you should not do when coaching is give the student you are coaching the answers. The student would not understand how they got to the answer and in a test, if a similar question came up they would not be able to understand how to get to the answer, and you would not be able to give it to them. When a person is coached, they feel a sense of accomplishment and are appreciative to the person who coached them. The coach will feel happy that they helped someone.

(Shannon)

Coaching is when your learning partner is stuck on a question and they need your guidance so you help them making sure they understand how and why you did those steps. I think it helps my learning because sometimes in mathematics I struggle and I need coaching to help me understand why and how I have gotten the answer wrong. I like being coached because I get the opportunity to learn from my mistakes and I like coaching because I like it when I get to see others getting their own opportunity to learn from their mistakes and the satisfaction of knowing you helped someone learn from their mistakes is amazing. A good learning coach doesn't tell their learning partner the answer.

(Amandeep)

A good learning coach doesn't tell them the answer but leads them to it by asking questions. A good learning coach doesn't give up when the student doesn't get the answer right. A good learning coach doesn't distract the person they are coaching by talking about unnecessary things.

(Mia)

Maddy Cooper, their teacher

The students are more in charge of their learning and the learning is more active. They have become learning resources for each other.

Sentence stems

Sarah Stevens and Paul Bloomberg, from The Core Collaborative, San Diego, devised the following peer conversation stems (Figure 4.3). The 'next steps' box encourages further thinking and discussion. The more we give students the words to use to become learning resources for one another, the more enabled and proficient they become.

Figure 4.3 Peer conversation stems

Mid lesson feedback stops: feedback for every student

Sadler's second and third stages of closing the gap – that students need to *'compare the actual level of performance with the goal'* and *'engage in appropriate action which leads to some closure of the gap'* – is again the focus of this section. The sections above have focused on ways in which students and teachers can get 'underneath the understanding' in order to facilitate effective feedback about their performance against the goal. Ongoing and mid lesson learning stops are integral to enabling the process of self-review, a striving to improve during the process and for students to see again examples of what excellence looks like, *thus providing feedback for everyone at the same time.* These are powerful pauses in the learning process, because they embody 'deliberate practice': specific identification of excellence and how, with examples or modeling, improvements can be made. This goes a long way to ensuring that feedback is given, received and then acted upon.

Teachers can stop at any time during a lesson and ask the class to analyze students' ongoing work projected on a screen, thus comparing their current learning with someone else's, after whole class analysis of excellent examples at the beginning of a lesson, or series of lessons. Random work is chosen, so that everyone is focused, not knowing whose work will be picked. Anybody's work can be discussed if the same process is used, whether the highest or the lower achiever is the author/mathematician/scientist or the like. The routine tends to be as follows:

---

1. The piece is projected on the screen. Ask the class to read through the piece first, look at it if art work, study it if mathematics and so on.
2. They decide, in pairs, what are the best bits, reflecting the success criteria and/or which elements have the greatest impact if narrative writing. As discussed in Chapter 3, a piece might have very few technical aspects but be brilliant in other ways. Students give their opinions about the best bits and these are underlined and analyzed as to why they are so good.
3. The class is then asked if there are any parts that could be improved or made even better, thinking of the purpose of the task and related success criteria. This might include vocabulary or punctuation changes for English, more justification or generalization in Science, points of error in Mathematics.

> *We don't want to improve things just for the sake of it. I once witnessed two students changing one really good sentence into a short sentence, taking out the good adjectives, simply because the success criteria listed short sentences for effect for a scary story. Students needing to develop 'a nose' for quality by exposure to wonderful sentences and phrases in excellent texts, so that they feel the quality rather than itemize it.*

This process models for students how to analyze and edit their own work and to collaborate to discuss and improve each other's work, identifying effective elements then giving ***specific suggestions for improvement.***

What are 'specific improvement suggestions'?

Ron Berger's famous 'Austin's Butterfly' YouTube clip (2013) has received global appreciation of **the value of meaningful and specific feedback** (e.g. *The wings need to be more pointy and more triangular)*, **rather than general feedback** *(e.g. Try to make the wings look better)*. Many teachers have shown this clip to their classes, emphasizing the importance of deliberate practice and specific improvement suggestions. Perhaps the greatest message of the video is the power of the collaborative approach, the public critique with clear guidelines given as to how the young student should give their comments so that Austin feels empowered rather than deflated. For those unfamiliar, here is a summary of the lesson, held in ANSER Charter school in Boise, Idaho, with a class of first graders (5/6-year-olds):

Austin chose a scientific illustration of a Western Swallowtail butterfly to copy (Figure 4.4) to make into a note card, something which was a whole school event, the finished note cards being printed and eventually sold in the community. Without sophisticated art and fine motor skills he began his first draft by looking at the photo, then putting it to one side as he drew the butterfly image he had in his head.

The teacher, Berger, then placed Austin's drawing (Figure 4.5) next to the photograph and, with the whole class, Austin was encouraged to think like a scientist and to observe carefully and record his observations. Austin's peers were asked to give him advice (helpful, specific and kind) about how he could change his drawing to more closely resemble the photo. First they focused on wing shape and when this was correct they moved on to wing pattern. The class had created a rubric for what quality would look like for both aspects:

Figure 4.4 Western swallowtail

Figure 4.5 First draft

Butterfly shape

Self-critique	Does not meet expectations	Almost meets expectations	Meets expectations
Does your butterfly fill the whole paper?	Does not fill even half the page.	Fills about ¾ of the page.	Drawing comes to almost 1 ½ inches of edges.

Self-critique	Does not meet expectations	Almost meets expectations	Meets expectations
Are the butterfly wings and the body in proportion to one another?	Wings and/or body are not in proportion.	Wings and body are somewhat in proportion.	Wings and body are closely in proportion.
Are the wings symmetrical?	Wings are not symmetrical.	One pair of wings are closely symmetrical.	Both pairs of wings are closely symmetrical.
Does the body include an abdomen, thorax, head and antennae?	Body has only 1 part and may have antennae.	Body has only 2 parts and may have antennae.	Body has 3 parts and antennae.

Butterfly pattern

Self-critique	Does not meet expectations	Almost meets expectations	Meets expectations
Observed markings ■ Eye spots ■ Borders ■ Stripes ■ Scallops ■ Veins ■ Splotches	Did not include observed markings.	Includes some observed markings.	Includes most observed markings.
Accurate drawing of markings	Did not accurately draw most markings.	Accurately drew some markings.	Accurately drew most markings.

It is worth pointing out at this stage, that these rubrics are typical of closed learning intention success criteria, as outlined in the previous chapter. Because it is a closed skill (to be able to copy this drawing/closely observe) the criteria are closed and compulsory. For a piece of writing, by contrast, a set of criteria do not operate in the same way – they are not compulsory but instead are a toolkit of possible strategies, and, on their own, unlike the butterfly criteria, do not guarantee quality. Nevertheless, the improvement suggestions for a piece of writing can be equally specific (e.g. 'You could say your heart was thumping instead of you were scared': giving the author ideas and stimulus).

The first graders first suggested that Austin should make the wing shape more pointy, more triangular and less round and that he should include the swallowtails at the bottom. He was pleased and went off to create draft 2 (Figure 4.6). The

Figure 4.6 Second draft

students next told Austin that this was much better but they reminded him that he had forgotten that butterflies have an upper and lower wing on each side.

At draft 3 (Figure 4.7) he was again praised for his progress but the students said that the upper wings had become round again, so he had to make the upper wings more pointy again.

Figure 4.7 Third draft

At draft 4 (Figure 4.8) the group told him he was now ready for the pattern. He carefully copied the pattern and produced draft 5 (Figure 4.9). He was then told he was ready for color and by matching the colors from the photograph produced the final draft (Figure 4.10).

Figure 4.8 Fourth draft   **Figure 4.9** Fifth draft   **Figure 4.10** Final draft

(Student artwork by Austin. 'Austin's Butterfly'. Courtesy of ANSER Charter School in Boise, ID, part of the EL Education network. View online at *Models of Excellence*. <http://modelsofexcellence.eleducation.org/projects/austins-butterfly-drafts>)

Not only was the finished product an example of beautiful work, it also signified the transformation of Austin as a small student drawing to a beginning scientist/artist.

The point of looking closely at what happened in 'Austin's Butterfly' is to see how important the specific and clear feedback is in illustrating deliberate practice in action and its impact on the development of the finished product. Had the feedback been less specific (e.g. *'You could make the wings better'*), it is likely that Austin would not have achieved this level of quality. More examples of Ron Berger's work can be found at www.modelsofexcellence. eleducation.org.

If we apply those specific improvement suggestions to student writing, for instance, it is clear that simply asking for 'a better sentence' or 'more evidence' is often not enough to really make a difference. It involves more effort to think of possible words, phrases or to give examples of what a student might include, but, without this, students would be justified in stating that if they had known how to improve it, they would have done it in the first place...

Self-improvements

After mid lesson learning stops, where some student work has been critiqued and analyzed, students are usually desperate to do some self-review and make improvements on their ongoing work, influenced and possibly inspired by the class discussion. It can be frustrating to be advised by a fellow student about errors or modifications which the student could have spotted if given the chance on their own first.

> Being forced to share partially completed or unedited work can make learners feel vulnerable in terms of the way their work will be viewed. By insisting their work is self-edited first, this will ensure that the feedback they receive points them in directions that they could not have discovered themselves and is key to them feeling confident about the work they are sharing.
>
> *(Costa & Garmston, 2017)*

Cooperative feedback discussions

At this point and/or when the learning is deemed finished, peer feedback can be a valuable source of sharing ideas for further improvement. In the past, the general interpretation of peer-marking or peer assessment has been the swapping of students' work. The student becomes a teacher, working on his or her own, making comments on the work about what they liked and what could be improved. Having seen many examples of pieces given comments by students in this way, the general impression has been that their comments tend to be superficial and relatively unhelpful. *Cooperative feedback*, in which the author has the last word and makes the improvements as a result of discussions with a learning partner, however, is an entirely different and more productive experience, a testament to the power of structured collaboration. Training students involves the following steps:

1. Both students read and discuss one of their pieces together, so **one book on top of the other**. The student whose work it is has control of the pen and ultimate say, unlike the swapping books scenario.
2. Together they decide the best bits, which they might disagree about, but reasons are given, and those bits underlined.
3. Then, together, they talk about improvements that could be made and the author makes them on the piece, there and then, writing the improvement often in a different color. As the available space for improvements will be limited, many schools leave the left-hand side of students' books blank, so that improvement can be written with no limits and retain legibility. No comments are written on the piece by either student, because this would take away precious time when the actual improvements could be made. Again, the author has the last word on the choice of improvement.
4. The students then go through the same process with their partner's work.
5. With older students and more complex work, they might then separate and attend to their improvements alone after the cooperative discussion.

Observations and video evidence of this process have revealed that:

a) *When the author reads their work out loud, pen in hand, they see their errors immediately. In the case of mathematics, the equivalent would be talk through their steps and their thinking, in line with the success criteria, with their partner.*
b) *Students have more natural conversations, interrupting each other or asking for clarification and so on, than when they are in a dialogue with a teacher.*

Becoming teachers for each other is a complex business so needs modeling and coaching. We need to make clear to students that their partner is only there to give them ideas, not to dictate and this should be modeled (*e.g. 'Thank you – that's made me think of another idea'*).

The cooperative improvement process can be used across all subjects. Instead of one 'book' on top of the other, they have one piece of mathematics, one piece of art work, one technology model and so on between them, so that they are not distracted, mid-conversation, to look at their own work.

This three-step practice of mid lesson stops followed by self-review then cooperative feedback discussions leads to students working much harder than they used to, compared to mainly uninterrupted work during lessons, with books handed in for copious marking by the teacher, given back at a later time when the feedback is too late to do anything about and is limited to written comments only. Of course, there are times when students should not be interrupted in their thinking, but when we are skill building, constant review is more helpful than waiting till the product is finished then needing to go back and redo it.

Feedback and feedforward

Stonefields School in Auckland, uses the terms 'feedback' and 'feedforward' to draw a distinction between what has been successful and what could be improved (www.stonefields.school.nz), although it should be noted that the term 'feedback' is usually defined as including both.

Figures 4.11 and 4.12 are examples of some of their resources.

Danielle de la Porte from Ross School, California, created the following feedback sentence stems for students to use when they were engaged in paired cooperative discussions about how each other's work or learning had been successful and how it could be improved.

Possible Feedback Sentence Starters for oral discussions

Positive comments

I really enjoyed/liked_____aspect because_____

I was impressed with_____because_____

I found_____part interesting/creative/informative

Constructive comments

I thought more detail/emphasis/creativity_____could have been applied to this part. For example_____

One aspect that I thought could be improved was _____.
To improve it I would suggest_____

The power of scheduled 1–1 conference sessions with students over one piece of work

A thousand words can be spoken between two people in a short time, with great impact because of the personal connection as well as the chance to truly understand what is being discussed, compared to the limitations of written feedback.

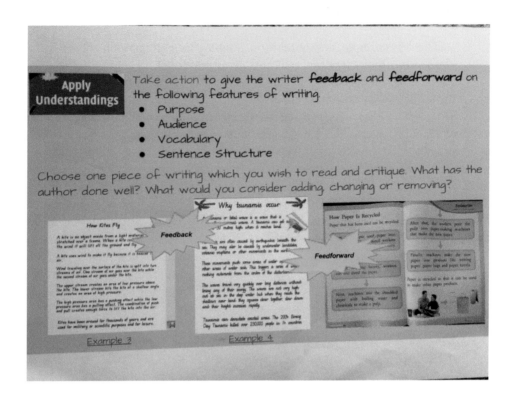

Figure 4.11 Applying understandings at Stonefields

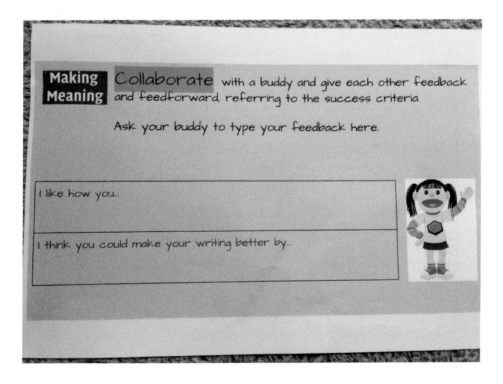

Figure 4.12 Buddy feedback at Stonefields

There is an increasing burden on teachers in many schools where there is an expectation that every piece should be responded to in some over detailed way. Because of this constraint, some teachers and schools are reducing the amount of times they write an improvement suggestion and replacing this with face to face 5–10 minute discussions with each student over a piece of their writing. Feedback so far suggests that this has greater benefits even if it can only be fitted in occasionally, than written improvement suggestions without that interaction. Clearly much can be said during such an exchange, not only about the learning, but also in developing the relationship between the teacher and student. Teachers typically say that students are very appreciative of the personal time allotted to them and feel valued because of this.

Maybe even a 3–5 minute talk together over a piece of writing, focusing, say, on the first few sentences, will have greater feedback benefits than a page of written comments. The power of face to face, personal, caring conversation with one student about the intricacies of how they might improve should not be underestimated. We believe these positive, constructive interactions are likely to be remembered by students for years to come.

Example of the possible discussion points in a face to face dialogue

The following piece of high level writing by a student from Herstmonceux School in Sussex is the first part of an unedited characterization. The success criteria were co-constructed by the class by analyzing a previous student's excellent characterization of a pirate. Notice the use of example phrases from that analyzed piece next to the success criteria to keep the meaning clear.

L.O. To write a character description (Author's intent – 007 character) – excerpt

Michael Striker was standing opposite Buckingham Palace waiting for his Rolex wristwatch to finally hit seven. He was a young man around 20 years old with a peculiar scar on his left cheek thanks to a gas explosion which was a gift from his last mission. His hair was wirey and a rich brown hat almost covered one of his beetle black eyes.

Michael was well built with broad soldier-like shoulders and a well-toned torso (as a result of his ruthless fitness regime). He wore a well pressed tuxedo and a bow tie, a bit like his hero 007, stylish and smart. Also he had a great sense of humoer like the time he stole the head teacher's wig and hid it from her whilst he was a student at Eton.

> ## Character description success criteria
> - Describe the face/hair/voice (e.g. tarry pigtail, scar on cheek).
> - Describe the body (e.g. big, broad shoulders).
> - Describe the clothes (e.g. soiled coat, stained apron).
> - 3rd person (e.g. he was, she is…).
> - Describe their actions (e.g. plodding heavily: show not tell).
> - Use a back story to help show their personality (e.g. he had a great sense of humor).
> - Likened to something (e.g. similes – 'sour as a gooseberry').

The impact of the piece on the reader is to provide an effective characterization, with the context of a 007 agent. Thinking of the impact on the reader helps direct any improvement suggestions:

Our feedback needs to be specific, helpful, kind and task rather than ego related, naming those parts where the impact on the reader has been successfully achieved: *'I like that you use the Rolex to show, not tell, how rich and successful he is. I also like the use of "finally" in the first sentence. It tells us that he has been waiting for a long time, rather impatiently, and for what? The reader's interest is alerted'.*

We might then suggest simply looking at how the punctuation could make the writing punchier, such as a dash between 'explosion' and 'a gift', removing the words 'which was'. We could ask if his name needs to appear – would it create more 007 impact if he remains anonymous? Could there be a sentence after the information about his watch waiting for seven, something which helps the reader see that he is on a dangerous mission perhaps? Would it have a sharper feel if 'was standing' became 'stood' and then similar verbs altered in the same way? Do we need wrist watch as well as Rolex? We would ask for the author's opinion, making clear that it is their decision each time, but getting him/her every time a suggestion is made to read that part aloud, to see if it does improve the writing or not.

Rebecca Tovell, a teacher of 6-year-olds at Peterhouse School, Norfolk, describes below how she organizes 1–1 conferences with her class.

1:1 feedback

For my weekly timetable, I have arranged a time slot on a Friday afternoon for me to be able to give feedback to each and every child on a piece of work that they have produced. During this time, I am able to meet with half of my class and spend roughly five minutes with each of them. The following week I will meet with the other half of the class. I normally only provide feedback on written work but previously I have feedback on math too.

Feedback structure

- The child and I talk about their feelings when doing the activity.
- I ask the child if they would like to read their work out loud or if they would prefer me to. We would identify any mistakes during this time.
- We discuss whether they achieved the learning objective and if they completed it independently or with adult support.
- The child and I use a green highlighter to identify the things they did well out of these symbols:

ABCDEFGHIJ KLMNOPQR STUVWXYZ capital letters	 finger spaces	 punctuation
  vocabulary	until yet but for because yet though conjunctions	 letter formation
  spelling	 presentation	 makes sense

- We underline any amazing sentences in green highlighter as well as draw a love heart at the end.
- We discuss what their next step should be and highlight the symbol in pink.
- When there are any spelling mistakes we talk about how to spell the word. Then I write the word in their book for them to copy. We also do this with any incorrect letter formation and sentences that do not make sense.

Impact

- In my last class I had twenty-nine out of thirty children who were able to write independently.
- Many of the learning gaps in children's writing were quickly closed.
- The progress from the start of (6-year-olds) to the end of the year was amazing. For example, a child with special needs who didn't achieve the expected standard in writing during their time in kindergarten, by the end of this year had securely met the writing criteria expected.
- Children enjoy marking their work with the teacher.
- It has helped to develop their self-esteem and build positive relationships with teacher.

Marking groups: 1–1 discussions within a group

Andy Silvester, from Crowmarsh School in Oxford, focuses on fewer pieces of writing in more depth with his class of 11-year-olds, ensuring that he has quality discussions with students in groups of four sharing their writing at each stage and discussing successes and possible improvements. The progress in students' books is evident on every page, as there are at least three drafts of every piece. Andy explains how he organizes this approach:

Marking groups

The overarching theme in my class is the central question, 'How is this piece of work significantly different from the last?' Everything in class is ultimately judged against that question meaning that the students are constantly challenged to justify their decisions and to find new ways to improve.

Summary structure:

A small group of students take it in turns to read a piece of work, discussing it and analysing it against set success criteria while the teacher guides conversation and marks the work. Targets are set for improvements and the group rotates round to the next piece of work. At the end of the discussion, students immediately edit their work in light of the new targets and assess the impact on their writing.

System in more detail

Prerequisite

Teaching takes place as normal, usually whole class. The shared class text is usually used as some form of stimulus alongside a good deal of discussion, teacher modeling, examples of good ones etc. to establish success criteria.

Marking groups

Structure

Once the work is underway, groups are set up in a rather fluid way, mixing abilities together in a way that I know will draw the best benefit for those involved. Groups range from 3–6 with 4 being ideal.

Process

Stage 1 – set up

To begin, the task is discussed and the success criteria analyzed so that the group know what evidence might look like. Each child then chooses a particular element to look out for, e.g. effective use of openers, variety of sentence structures, the impact of the opening sentence, whatever is relevant to the task at the time.

Stage 2 – professional check

The first student's work is then displayed in front of the group and given the professional check which looks at the layout and general presentation. Is it appropriate for 11-year-olds?

The work is then read out and analyzed a section at a time, with students chipping in with comments particularly related to the criteria they choose to look out for in stage 1.

Stage 3 – analysis

Through discussion such as this and guided by the teacher, the group establish what they like about the work and a couple of targets needed to improve it. These are recorded at the end of the work and the group rotates to the next student.

Each time a student is given targets, they will then look out for those elements in the following pieces of work (see stage 1), judging the impact when they are present or absent as well as obtaining tips on how to achieve the target through example or discussion.

Timings: I would usually allow about 10 minutes per student.

While this process is taking place, I am not only facilitating the discussion, but also closely following along making notes either mentally or shorthand on the grammar and structure of the work which may not be so important to the rest of the group, but which will help me to inform personal targets at the end of the work in stage 3. This is recorded on the ongoing assessment sheets devised within the school meaning that the assessment system is up to date and an integral part of planning for next steps.

Stage 4 – edits

Immediately following the marking group, the students return to their desks and begin to edit their work in line with the advice they have been given, which in my mind is just as important as the advice that has been given in the first place. Advice followed by action creates habit and change.

Students often 'bolt on' to a marking group and are encouraged to do so if they feel it would be of benefit to them. They often do this to help them get past a sticking point by collecting some new ideas or because they are working on a target but need more guidance to achieve it. As a bolt on they are not directly involved in the conversation but are welcome to ask questions and respond to the discussion although their work will probably not be directly analyzed.

Stage 5 – self-assessment

Self-assessment is a key part of the process which can take two formats:

- The first is to complete the edits and then to assess the impact of the changes, explaining how and why the work is significantly improved.
- The second is to incorporate the edits into their self-assessment by identifying an element that needs to be improved, explaining how that could be achieved, editing the work and then explaining the impact.

The self-assessment is a key element to the whole structure that helps me as a teacher to understand the depth of their understanding regarding the target which in turn helps to guide future planning and personal target setting.

Summary

At the end of this process the entire class will have been through a marking group at least once for each piece of work but quite possibly twice if time runs well (once while it has been underway and once at the end) and quite possibly returned as a bolt on at some later date. I consider that the marking has been completed and so do not take books away from the class for marking. Ever.

The process is time consuming and requires a rethink as to how the timetable is constructed. Typically, a full cycle of marking groups from the beginning of the work to the end of the self-assessment phase could take a good couple of weeks. I find that I complete fewer total pieces of work throughout the year than by taking the traditional approach, but consider that the depth of the learning and the level of improvements far outweigh this.

The examples (Figures 4.13 and 4.14) from two students illustrate the power of the marking groups approach:

> The context was a short analysis of the novel 'Daughter of the Sea' by Bernie Doherty. The focus of the teaching was to develop sophistication in writing by developing a more cinematic approach, starting off with broad details before becoming more focused.

Student 1

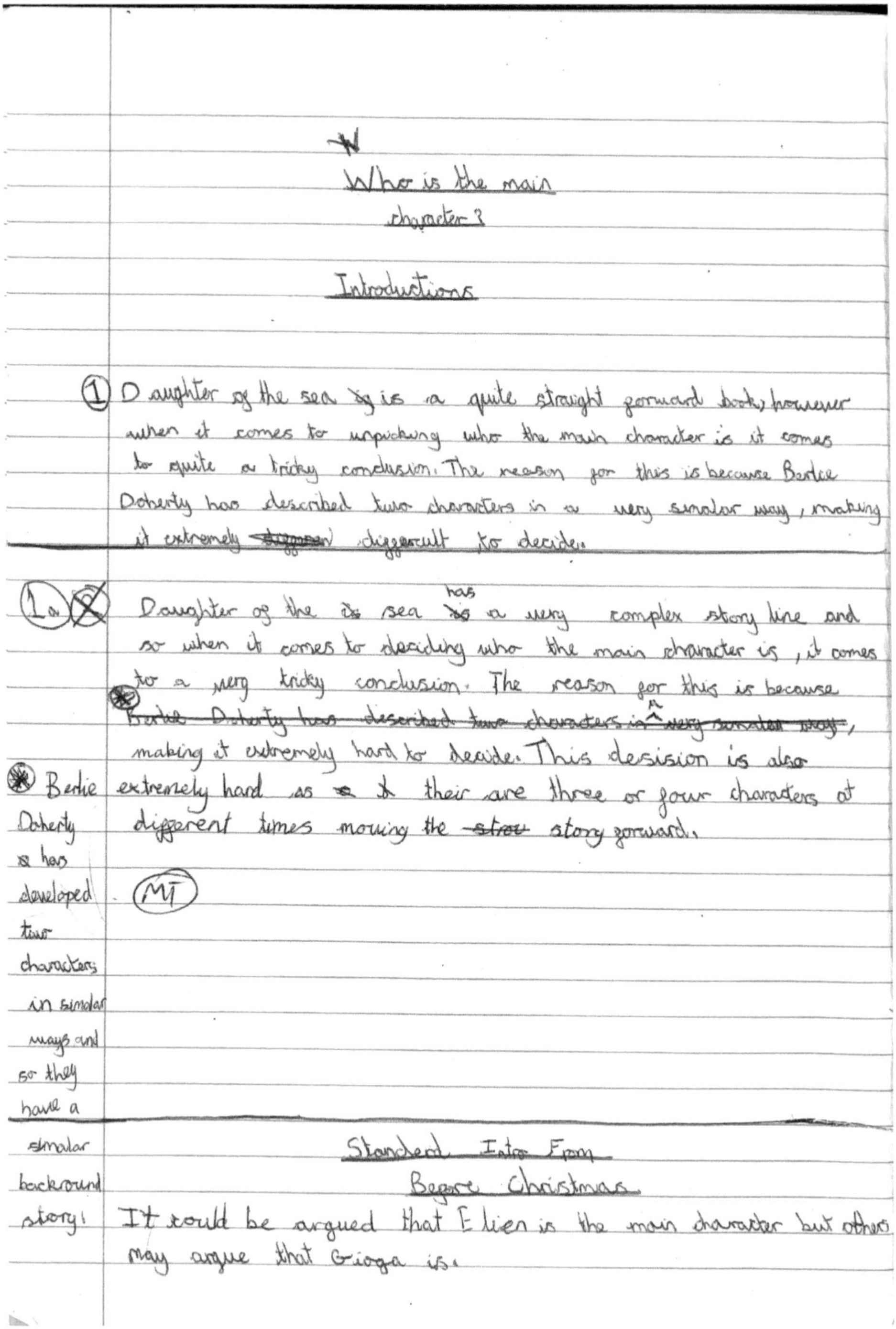

Who is the main
character?

Introductions

① Daughter of the sea *by* is a quite straight forward book, however when it comes to unpicking who the main character is it comes to quite a tricky conclusion. The reason for this is because Bertie Doherty has described two characters in a very similar way, making it extremely ~~different~~ difficult to decide.

(1a) ✗   has
Daughter of the ~~is~~ sea ~~is~~ a very complex story line and so when it comes to deciding who the main character is, it comes to a very tricky conclusion. The reason for this is because ~~Bertie Doherty has described two characters in a~~ ~~very similar way~~, making it extremely hard to decide. This desision is also

✱ Bertie   extremely hard as ~~a~~ ~~t~~ their are three or four characters at
Doherty   different times moving the ~~stroe~~ story forward.
✗ has
developed   (MT)
two
characters
in similar
ways and
so they
have a
similar
backround   Standerd Into From
story.   Before Christmas
              It could be argued that Elien is the main character but others
              may argue that Grioga is.

Figure 4.13 Student 1

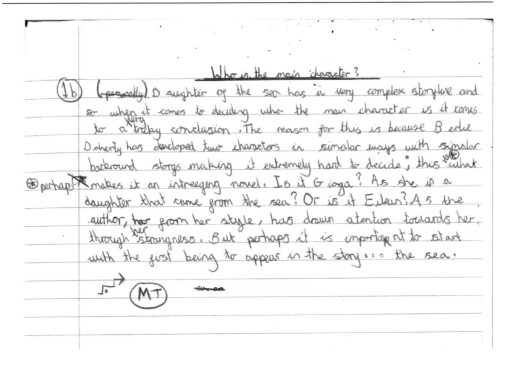

Figure 4.13 (continued)

Transcript

Drafts 1 and 1a were completed in a small mixed ability group, sharing ideas.

Draft 1: **Daughter of the Sea is a quite straight forward book, however when it comes to unpicking who the main character is it comes to quite a tricky conclusion. The reason for this is because Bernie Doherty has described two characters in a very similar way, making it extremely difficult to decide.**

Draft 1a: **Daughter of the sea has a very complex story line and so when it comes to deciding who the main character is, it comes to a very tricky conclusion. The reason for this is because Bernie Doherty has developed two characters in simaler ways and so they have a similar background story, making it extremely hard to decide. This decision is also extremely hard as there are three or four characters at different times moving the story forward.**

MT (Marked together) in a marking group with the teacher then takes place with the following advice given:

■ *Contextualize the characters to explain why they were options*

Draft 1b (final): **Daughter of the Sea has a very complex storyline and so when it comes to deciding who the main character is it comes to a**

very tricky conclusion. The reason for this is because Bernie Doherty has developed two characters in very similar ways with similar background storys making it extremely hard to decide; this is what perhaps makes it an intreeging novel. Is it Gioga? As she is a daughter that comes from the sea? Or is it Eileen? As the author, from her style, has drawn attention towards her through her strangeness. But perhaps it is important to start with the first being to appear in the story...the sea.

A second MT session followed in which the finished product was shared and celebrated.

Student 2

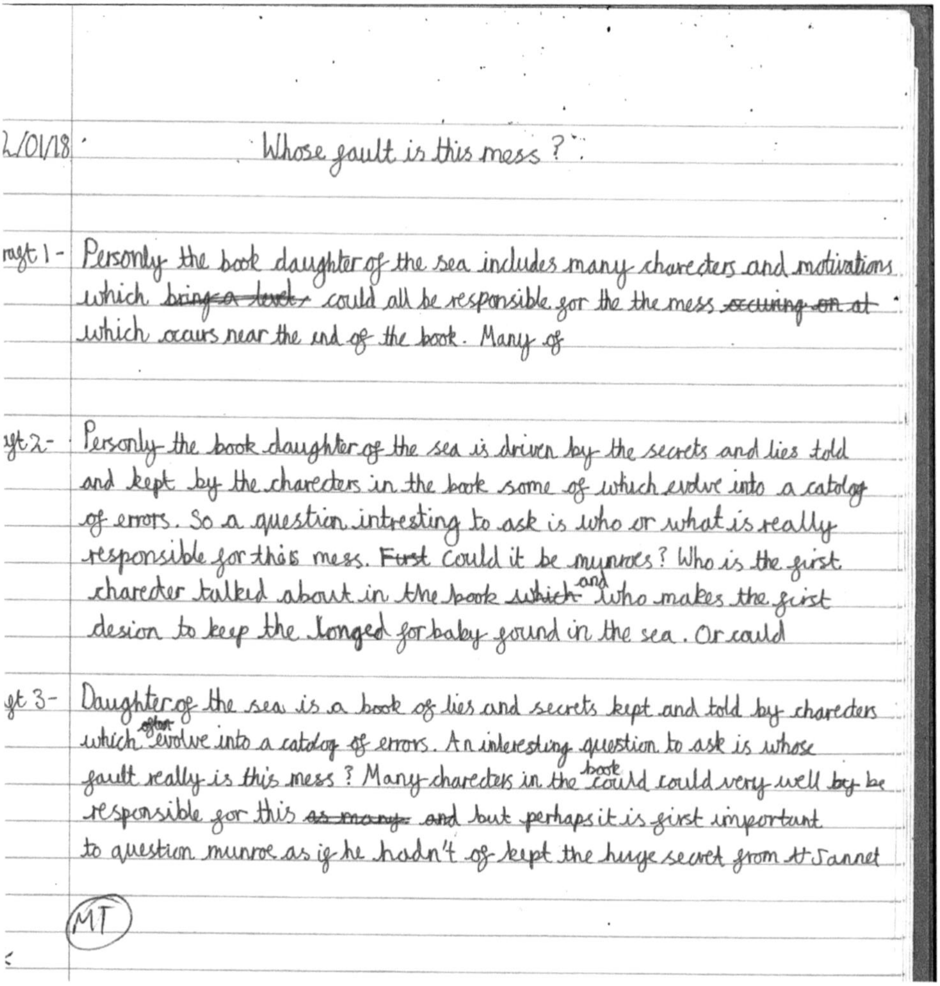

2/01/18 Whose fault is this mess?

mpt 1 - Personly the book daughter of the sea includes many charecters and motivations which ~~bring a level~~ could all be responsible for the the mess ~~occuring on at~~ which occurs near the end of the book. Many of

pt 2 - Personly the book daughter of the sea is driven by the secrets and lies told and kept by the charecters in the book some of which evolve into a catalog of errors. So a question intresting to ask is who or what is really responsible for this mess. ~~First~~ Could it be munroe? Who is the first charecter talked about in the book ~~which~~ and who makes the first desion to keep the longed for baby found in the sea. Or could

pt 3 - Daughter of the sea is a book of lies and secrets kept and told by charecters which often evolve into a catalog of errors. An interesting question to ask is whose fault really is this mess? Many charecters in the book could could very well ~~by~~ be responsible for this ~~as many~~ and but perhaps it is first important to question munroe as if he hadn't of kept the huge secret from St Jannet

MT

Figure 4.14 Student 2

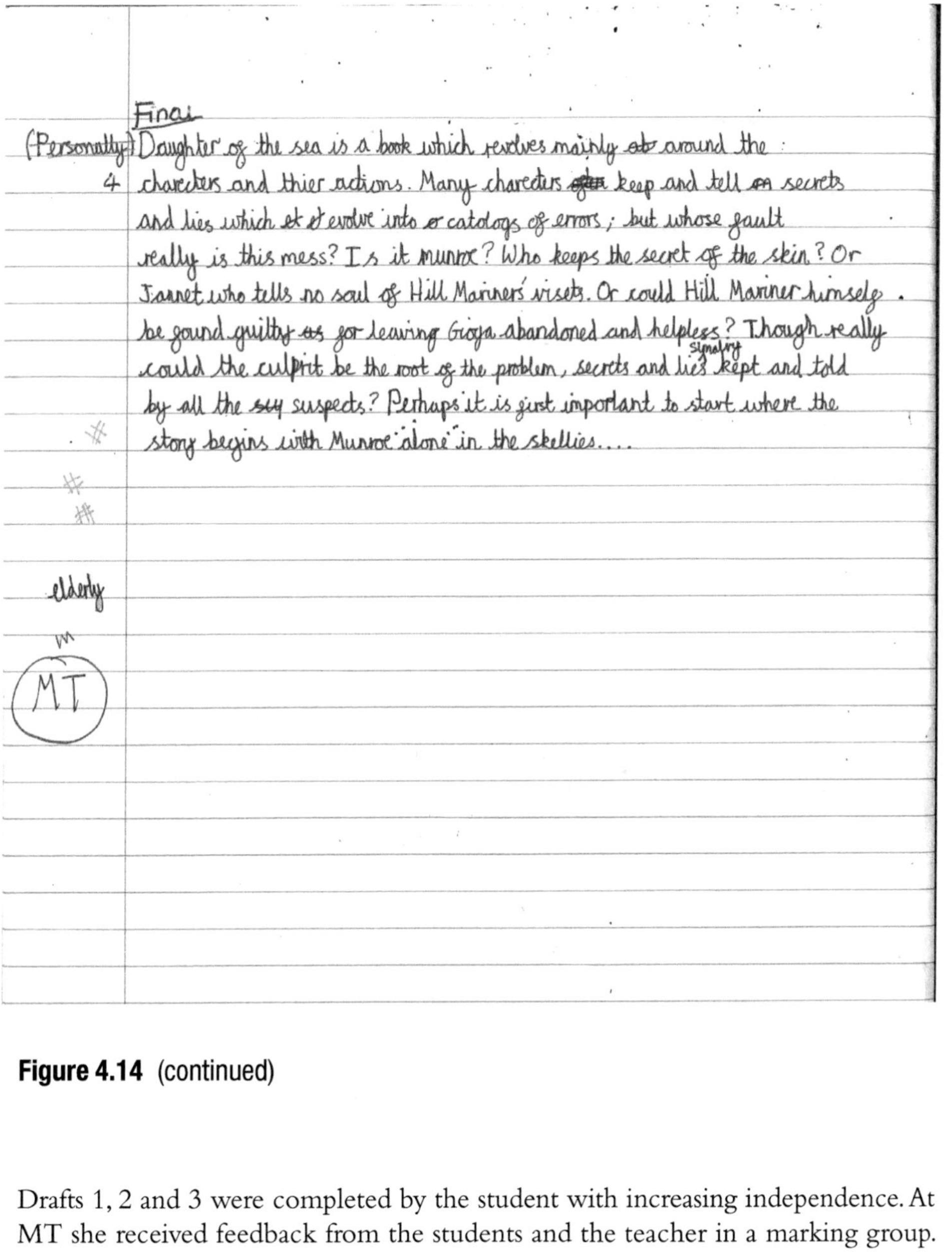

Final

(Personally) Daughter of the sea is a book which revolves mainly ot around the
4 | characters and thier actions. Many charecters offe keep and tell on secrets
and lies which et ot evolve into or catalogs of errors ; but whose fault
really is this mess? I s it munroe ? Who keeps the secret of the skin ? Or
Jannet who tells no soul of Hill Mariners visets. Or could Hill Mariner himself .
be found guilty as for leaving Gioja abandoned and helpless ? Though really
could the culprit be the root of the problem, secrets and lies kept and told
by all the six suspects? Perhaps it is first important to start where the
story begins with Munroe alone in the skellies....

elderly

MT

Figure 4.14 (continued)

Drafts 1, 2 and 3 were completed by the student with increasing independence. At MT she received feedback from the students and the teacher in a marking group. Advice given:

- *contextualize characters to explain why they were options,*
- *consider creating a link to the next paragraph.*

Her final paragraph was then written independently.

One of the key features of Andy's writing lessons is that as each draft is completed, he photocopies them and places them in a hanging plastic wallet in the classroom. Students are encouraged to take these out of the wallet to read each other's drafts, thus seeing multiple examples of excellence and different styles, word choices and so on. Notice the influence the two writers have had on one another above, with both ending 'Perhaps it is important to start….' and including questions to intrigue the reader.

4. Conclusions

a) Principles

The short answer to this myriad of research findings and classroom strategies is that we need to want to know our students and their learning, to have them trust us and know that we have their best interests at heart. Feedback cannot be led by a simple formula, because students are all different and need different approaches. There seem to be, however, some fundamental principles of in the moment feedback to aim for, within the knowledge that in the moment feedback has the greatest impact:

- Encourage challenge and struggle as the norm when in the learning process.
- Make learning purposeful where possible.
- Point out misconceptions and use them as opportunities for self-correction.
- Provide feedback opportunities between students.
- Make all feedback task related (learning intention, success criteria) rather than ego related (how smart they are).
- Don't give feedback too quickly, too often or at the expense of the cognitive demand…allow more struggle, climbing out of the pit, and less reliance on it… but know the student.
- Give and encourage feedback which is just right for each student (not too easy, not too challenging).

b) Timing

The timing of any learning and feedback strategies is a crucial component in determining their level of success. The following table summarizes what we know works best:

Stage of learning	What is needed
Lesson/unit start	<ul><li>Students' confidence in understanding and valuing the lesson/s.</li><li>An overview of what success might look like.</li><li>Related learning intentions and success criteria.</li></ul>

Stage of learning	What is needed
Acquiring surface learning	■ Know how to summarize, outline and relate the learning to prior achievement.
Consolidation of surface learning	■ Engaging deliberate practice, rehearsing over time and learning how to seek and receive feedback.
Acquiring deep understanding	■ Planning and evaluation, monitoring own learning strategies.
Consolidating deep understanding	■ Know how to and engage in self-talk, self-evaluate, self-questioning, seeking help from peers. ■ Transfer learning to new situations, which involves knowing how to detect similarities and differences between old and new.

Whether and how students respond to our feedback is, of course, the only thing that matters, or we could simply be wasting our time. As Dylan Wiliam says (Wiliam and Leahy, 2015), *'The most effective feedback is just feedback that our students actually use in improving their learning'*.

Key points

- The level of student self-efficacy affects the way in which they receive feedback.
- Tasks should have a level of 'desirable difficulties' to maximize achievement.
- Forgetting helps us remember better when the content is revisited.
- Spaced, not massed learning is more effective.
- Sometimes less feedback is more, to encourage more problem solving and use of 'stuck' strategies.
- The more meaningful the context the more likely the learning is to be remembered.
- Student to teacher feedback is most important and consists of a) Where am I going? b) How am I going? and c) Where to next?/How can it be improved?
- Searching questioning and listening to paired student discussions reveals student understanding.
- Don't assume you know what is happening when asking a student about their work – seek feedback from the student about what they think is going on.
- Misconceptions and slips should be treated differently.
- Students should be activated as learning resources for one another.
- Peer coaching needs training and modeling.

- Mid lesson learning stops, in which student work is projected mid flow for class analysis for successes and improvements, giving specific suggestions, is a powerful tool for a) enabling instant feedback for all and b) modeling the process which students in pairs can then carry out.
- Knowing the best time to give feedback is key to its success (e.g. when consolidating deep understanding is optimal time for peer discussions).

CHAPTER

5

Post-lesson feedback

Our focus for the most powerful feedback was covered in the previous chapter 'The power of within: lesson verbal feedback'. **Anything which happens after the lesson has questionable value compared to what happens in the moment,** yet teachers are often bogged down with copious books to mark, grade or write comments for after lessons, much of which has limited value in helping students to progress. It is our intention to attempt to ease teachers' workload by emphasizing that often *less is more* when it comes to post-lesson feedback.

This chapter deals firstly with: a) the feedback we can gather from students at the end of lessons to inform us about next steps, both in our teaching and their learning, then tackles the thorny issue of b) teacher to student feedback via grading. We then move on to explore issues about c) written comment feedback, and give examples of different marking strategies used by teachers. Finally, d) feedback not directly linked to individual lessons, often summative, and including parents or other school partners will be discussed followed by e) examples of excellent feedback policies and comments by the school leaders.

a) Feedback from student to teacher after lessons

Student voice

As stated in our first chapter, the importance of the feedback students give teachers, in its many forms, is our starting point when determining the nature of our subsequent feedback to them. In our dilemma over coverage, it seems that student voice is often sacrificed for lack of time. Alison Peacock, in her book *Assessment for Learning without Limits*, cites Luke Rolls, a teacher at the University of Cambridge School, who, for his higher degree, interviewed some 9-year-olds in a London school about their experience of mathematics lessons. Their responses show the value of finding ways of hearing what students think about our teaching, their learning, and what it is to be them:

Luke:　How does that feel when you say the lessons are rushing?

Gina:　I don't like that. I actually come to school to learn. I don't like it when we do one lesson on adding fractions and then one lesson on something completely different. I actually want to learn it a few times to get it in my head, not just once.

Permjit expresses his frustration about the apparent lack of time in many classrooms for ideas to be expressed and debated:

> The thing is with teachers, they try to say everything and so you don't have time. I'm not pointing to you Mr. Rolls . . . but the teachers, they could say less, for the students to say more. They do know a lot, but they should say less, because let's say it was them ten years before, they wouldn't want their teacher to say everything because they would want to be learning. You're not really learning that much because the teacher's just giving you everything . . . Arguing is good because you are taking on people's ideas and then it helps you understand. Basically, you should say what you think, see what people say and then think about it.
>
> *(Alison Peacock, 2016)*

If we can hear this kind of honest feedback from students we have a much greater chance of making the learning visible, as we see what it means to be in their shoes. In these two statements from students, we see implied deliberate practice, spaced teaching, overlearning and active rather than passive learners with the student doing more of the talking, thinking and learning. These are known effective strategies, which these students know without the benefit of research evidence!

Langford School, in Fulham, has a 'Langford Listener' assigned to every student in the school. This person is not their class teacher and includes every adult in the school – even the janitor, administrative staff, school business manager and so on. Children meet in groups with their assigned adult to discuss how life in general is at the school, what they are enjoying and what feedback they would like to give to the teachers. A form is completed by the adult to report anything back from the discussion. Students also know they can find their 'Langford Listener' at any time and speak to them privately.

Many schools also have a post-box, usually outside the school leader's room, for children to write a signed or anonymous note to him or her about anything troubling them, and, if signed, they always need to receive and get a personalized response. Some examples from Langford:

Dear Mr. Gibbons,

I am writing to inform you that a tap in the boys' toilet when you put it on it runs for a long time. I know you're busy but couldn't you do something about it.

By Omar Team 5

Thanks for reading this letter.

Dear Mr. Gibbons,

I would like to discuss a matter of the utmost importance. In my class if a minority of people are misbehaving the majority is badly affected. This started to occur when classes were no longer a class but a team.

On the back of that if a majority have to be punished for what the minority have done, if the minority is rewarded then logically the majority should be rewarded too.

However, I would like to congratulate you for a magnificent start at Langford School.

Yours sincerely

P

Dear Mr. Gibbons,

I am writing to you that I am being bullied by a girl named Mia. I am in Year 6 and she's been doing this for so long. I'm trying to ignore her but she won't stop bullying me. Can you please do something about this. I don't feel happy.

Yours sincerely,

Souha K

Student evaluations of lessons and their learning

Students from Mount Waverley Secondary College in Melbourne, recently embarked on a project to improve teacher student relationships, 'Teach the Teacher', under the supervision of Hayley Dureau, the Leading Teacher for Student Voice. The students surveyed their peers and decided (based on the survey results) to focus their attention on student-to-teacher feedback. In the same year the students ran professional learning sessions for the teachers and school leaders in which they worked together with their teachers to create a student-to-teacher feedback survey that could be used by teachers at any year level (7–12) and in any subject area. The next year the resulting survey was rolled out across the whole college.

In 2017 the teachers once again used the survey, with an emphasis now on using the data collected to improve teacher practice. The 'Teach the Teacher' team again ran sessions with staff, discussing how the teachers could use the information in their practice (for instance, if the teacher thought they were communicating clearly but the data suggested otherwise, the students suggested strategies for improving their communication, which in many cases were strategies that the teachers themselves had not considered). The students also encouraged teachers to share strategies with one another, especially where the survey results were very positive for any particular teacher. An excerpt from the students' findings by Netania and Chester:

How much influence do teachers really have on student learning?

Teachers, according to research, have the most impact on student learning, after the students themselves. Whereas it can be hard for teachers to help students who have no intention of learning, their ability to influence students was generally higher than any other factor, such as parents or the school environment.

How did our surveys help?

Our surveys helped determine the general attitude of the students. The results from our surveys consolidated the fact that students feel that a healthy relationship with their teachers is crucial to their success, and even though they feel their teachers are there to help, they do not feel comfortable enough to approach them.

Our teacher surveys highlighted the passion teachers possess towards their job and their overwhelming desire to help their students. They also echoed the students' message about the need for healthy student-teacher relationships.

There was also some similarity between the survey results of the students and the teachers. For example, teachers said they try to be as approachable as possible, yet students felt they were not in many cases.

After an extensive project on feedback, students were surveyed again, saying that they 'can see a huge improvement in the way teachers teach now'. 'It has made everyone realize that it is possible for students to talk to teachers and give them feedback and it doesn't have to be in a negative light' and 'It's nice for the teacher to hear the good stuff once in a while but constructive criticism is good too'.

A number of teachers have recently experimented with asking students' opinions about how well lessons went, with illuminating feedback. Note – they focus on impact on student learning. Figures 5.1, 5.2 and 5.3 from Katherine Muncaster in Ludworth School, Stockport reveal some of their thinking: the first student wants a private desk, the second wants her to go over long division and the third asks for more challenging work.

Liz Brough from St. Peter's Primary School in Galashiels asked students, 'What did I do that helped you understand?' and 'What could I have done to help you understand it better?' She began trialling with just two questions, as seen in Figure 5.4.

Feedback

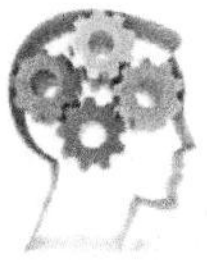

Has your learning improved so far in Year 6? How?

Yes because at the begining of the year I knew very littl but now I see a massive difference.

How has your teacher helped you to learn?

I think my teacher has helped me to learn by making me sit next to the appropriate people which helps me learn.

What could your teacher do differently to help you learn?

I think my teacher can help me better by giving each person their own little table (like a desk).

Anything else....

Figure 5.1 Student to teacher feedback

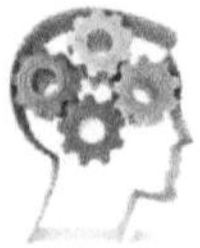

Feedback

Has your learning improved so far in Year 6? How?

Yes, I am feeling more confident in maths and English. I also feel more confident in spelling.

How has your teacher helped you to learn?

By teaching me things that I was unsure about. By helping me and encouraging me to do well and not give up.

What could your teacher do differently to help you learn?

Go over long division.

Anything else....

Figure 5.2 Student to teacher feedback

Feedback

Has your learning improved so far in Year 6? How?

Yes. Because my confidence has improved a lot and I feel more comfortable in lessons.

How has your teacher helped you to learn?

My teacher has let me show my specialities. Especially in things like the production and in whose got talent?

What could your teacher do differently to help you learn?

They could've uped the level of the work because sometimes I find it a bit easy.

Anything else....

Figure 5.3 Student to teacher feedback

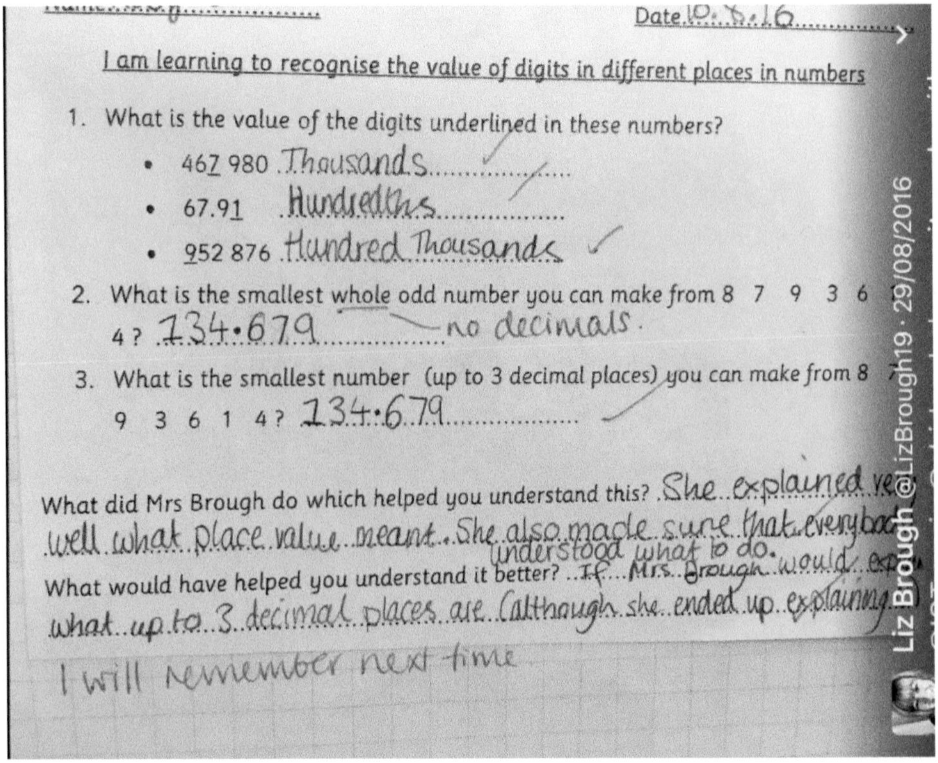

Figure 5.4 Student to teacher feedback

Liz Brough then developed a sheet in which she listed the possible helpful aspects, so that she could get a better idea about which of her strategies were working best (Figure 5.5). The student would like more diagrams to help her understand.

Liz's reflections about seeking student feedback:

> This has impacted my teaching by focusing me – I have tried to take on board the students' suggestions for how I could have helped them learn better by molding the delivery of a lesson into the way they learn best. I think it's also impacted the students because they feel more ownership of their learning.

Liz also uses the 'text message' question (Figure 5.6) to her at the end of the lesson, asking for what she could do to help them with their mathematics.

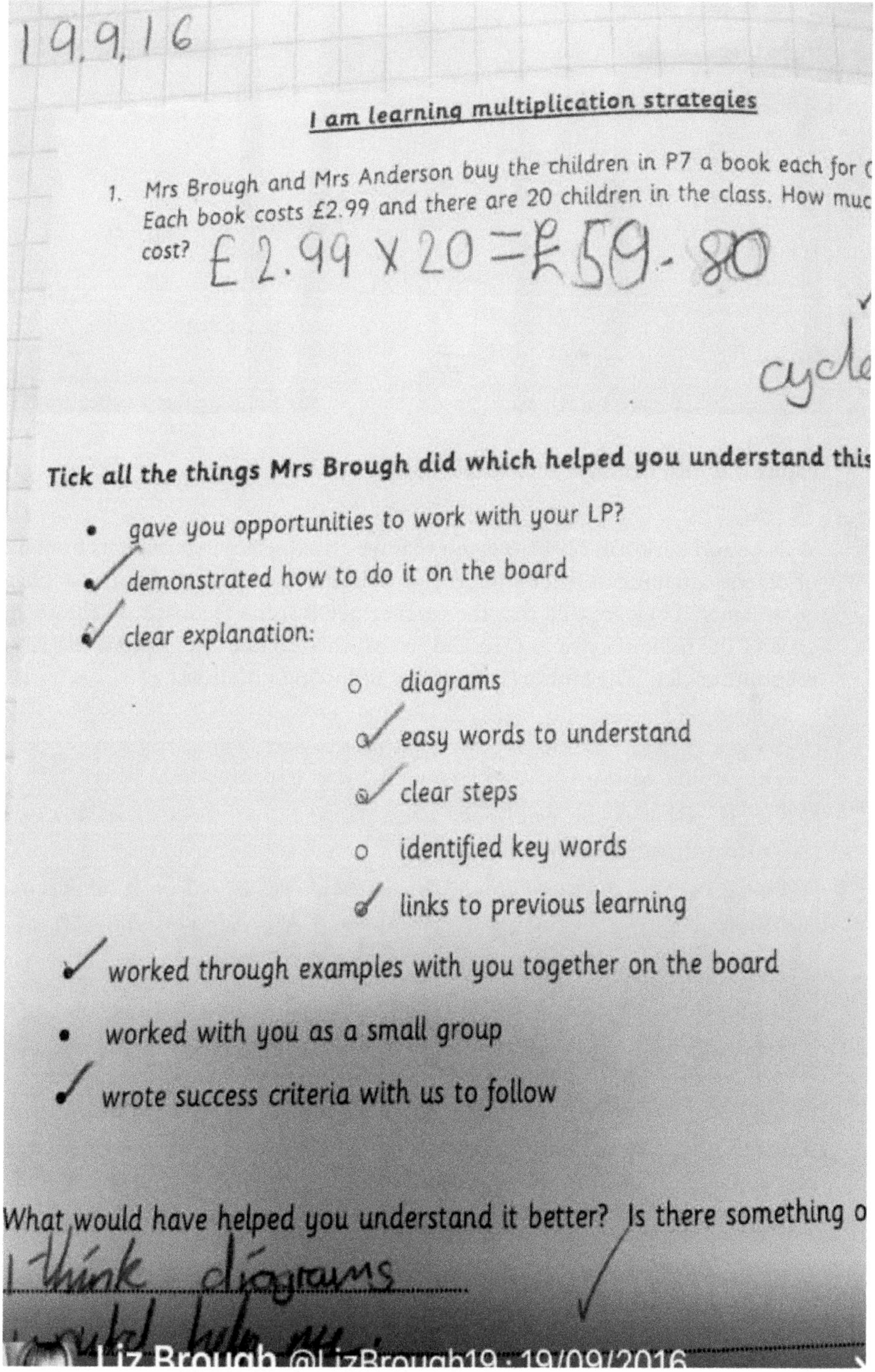

19.9.16

<u>I am learning multiplication strategies</u>

1. Mrs Brough and Mrs Anderson buy the children in P7 a book each for (
   Each book costs £2.99 and there are 20 children in the class. How muc
   cost? £ 2.99 x 20 = £ 59.80

cycle

Tick all the things Mrs Brough did which helped you understand this

- gave you opportunities to work with your LP?

✓ demonstrated how to do it on the board

✓ clear explanation:

       o   diagrams

       ✓   easy words to understand

       ✓   clear steps

       o   identified key words

       ✓   links to previous learning

✓ worked through examples with you together on the board

- worked with you as a small group

✓ wrote success criteria with us to follow

What would have helped you understand it better? Is there something o

I think diagrams

would help me

Liz Brough @LizBrough19 · 19/09/2016

Figure 5.5 Student to teacher feedback

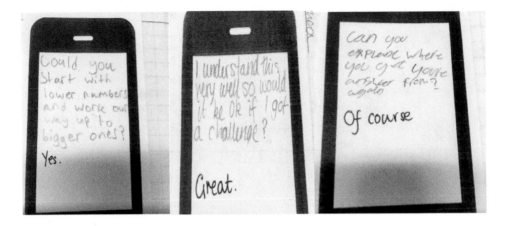

Figure 5.6 Text message student feedback

Wallace and Kirkman (2017) suggest that we could select five students from a class, of diverse attainments, background and attitude, and appoint them as a 'board of consultants'. They are told that the teacher needs some feedback on their experience of the topic they've just studied so that the teacher can improve the learning for a future class. The authors suggest the following questions:

> **Which part of the topic did you find most interesting? Why?**
>
> **Which part did you find least interesting? How could I make it more interesting for another class?**
>
> **What aspects of the topic do you remember best? Why do you think that is?**
>
> **Which activities or tasks helped you to learn best?**
>
> **Which parts of the topic did you struggle to understand?**
>
> **Was there an aspect of the topic you wish we'd had more time to explore?**
>
> **If you were going to teach this topic to someone else, how would you do it?**

Teachers from Clarke's learning team from Hertfordshire, trialling formative assessment strategies for 2016, also experimented with exit cards, which they said gave students the opportunity to:

- demonstrate their learning,
- summarize key points of a lesson,
- apply their learning to a new context,
- ask questions or explain how they feel about their learning.

Examples of exit cards can be seen at Figure 5.7.

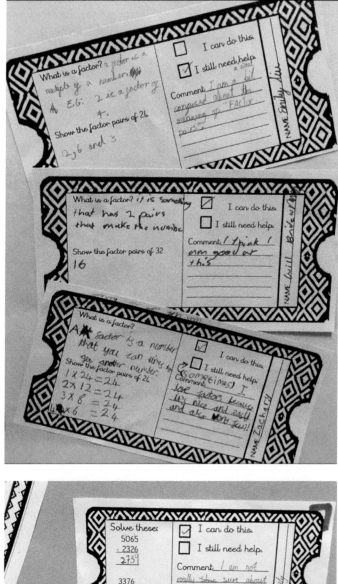

Figure 5.7 Exit cards

Teacher quotes

I can quickly spot which students still have misconceptions and provide immediate support, before they leave the lesson

It provides me with information about all the students in the class, rather than just a small group.

It enables me to know if my planning for the next lesson needs to be adapted and how.

I can give immediate reassurance or a well needed confidence boost to students who have concerns about their learning.

Student quotes

I like exit cards because they tell you if you're confident at what you are doing now.

I like exit cards because the teacher can know if you are struggling.

I like exit cards because it tells my teacher if I'm comfortable with my lesson or not. I also like them because it makes me think about my learning.

Jo Boaler (2016), in her book 'Mathematical Mindsets', describes how two teachers from the Vista Unified School District in California, Yekaterina Milvidskaia and Tina Tebelman, developed a set of homework reflection questions that the teachers choose from each day to help their students process and understand the mathematics they have met that day at a deeper level. These questions also give important feedback information to teachers about their students' thinking and could be more useful than more practice of the skill in focus. **One reflection question is assigned each night.** The reflection questions:

1. What were the main mathematical concepts or ideas that you learned today or that we discussed in class today?
2. What questions do you still have about . . .? If you don't have a question, write a similar problem and solve it instead.
3. Describe a mistake or misconception that you or a classmate had in class today. What did you learn from this mistake or misconception?
4. How did you or your group approach today's problem or problem set? Was your approach successful? What did you learn from your approach?
5. Describe in detail how someone else in class approached a problem. How is their approach similar or different to the way you approached the problem?
6. What new vocabulary words or terms were introduced today? What do you believe each new word means? Give an example/picture of each word.
7. What was the big mathematical debate about in class today? What did you learn from the debate?
8. How is . . . similar or different to . . .?
9. What would happen if you changed . . .?

> **10. What were some of your strengths and weaknesses in this unit? What is your plan to improve in your areas of weakness?**

b) Teacher to student post-lesson feedback

Grading

As Alfie Kohn (1994) said, *'Never grade students while they are still learning'* as so often such grading carries the message 'the work is over'. This encapsulates the key problem about grading student work. When a grade is assigned, students care about how they have done compared to others, thus receiving ego-related feedback, which damages learning. Like ability grouping, grading leads to students being defined by their grade ('I'm an A student'). Studies show that grading decreases student achievement, although, as stated earlier in this book, it is their overuse and lack of interpretation that can assist in subsequent learning that causes the problems, meaning there is still a place for summative grades used less frequently. When grading is summative (i.e. at the end of a topic or program), it can and does provide a judgment of the alignment of the student's work to the expected standard.

The major issue is whether or not there are improvement suggestions or 'where to next' comments in the feedback – and the opportunity to use this feedforward information. If there are none, learning is rarely enhanced, but similarly, if comments do not include this vital information, they can be just as useless.

In Ruth Butler's seminal 1988 experiment with the 12-year-olds (as noted in the first chapter of this book), four classes were graded, four classes received written comment only feedback and another four classes received both grades and comments. Those who received the comment only feedback did significantly better in a second test, those who received a grade performed worse the second time and the very worst performance, surprisingly, came from the classes which had received both grades and comments. Where even positive comments accompanied grades, interviews with students revealed that they believed the teacher was 'being kind' and that the grade was the real indicator of the quality of their work. Again, our main focus should be giving helpful, constructive feedback rather than sending confusing messages that the work is over.

Grading is a summative judgment and should, therefore, be held back until the end of the particular coverage when there has been a chance for students to progress through the learning without losing heart or becoming complacent. When the focus is a constructive, task related comment, the learner can then concentrate on making improvements and thus enhance their learning journey.

c) Written feedback

This section first deals with comment only feedback, what it might look like and how it works best, then other strategies, for giving written or otherwise feedback as a result of perusing student work, are explored.

Use cautiously . . .

Writing a worthwhile comment on every student's work would be a daunting task, and for teachers who have attempted this, an unmanageable workload results. It seems important that students know that we have looked at their work, but there are various strategies for giving feedback as well as comment feedback, which is the most time consuming.

The most powerful feedback, as emphasized in the previous chapter, is the 'in the moment' feedback, verbal or written, which teachers engage in throughout a lesson. When there have been mid lesson learning stops, in which all are given feedback via the analysis of a random work in progress, where students have self and peer improved and edited their work, a further written improvement suggestion by the teacher seems tokenistic. It must be stressed, however, that the practice of attempting this written improvement suggestions for every piece of work can be a waste of time which could otherwise be spent on planning the next lesson. Neither is it advisable, as often promoted in some schools and systems, to dictate a weekly 'deep mark', but instead to write these improvement comments only when the process of review and editing did not take place within the lesson, such as with a piece of completely unaided writing.

Improving the current piece . . .

In the past the term 'next steps' has led teachers to write comments advising student 'Next time, remember to . . .' which can also be a waste of time, as the advice might not be remembered at a later date, in a different context, especially for elementary aged students. For secondary students, advice about future work can be very informative, although we would still argue that the process of making improvements on existing work enables the student to not see the first attempt as the finished product but instead to rethink, refine and possibly redraft, so that this process becomes a natural habit. Suggesting improvements to the current piece of work, in the moment or very soon after it has been completed (e.g. Can you describe the chaos you mentioned in this sentence – give some examples), is more likely to extend the learning beyond the boundaries of the lesson and is more likely to be applied to later learning. These suggestions are particularly relevant for any written English work.

In Clarke (2005) suggestions were given for the different levels of support that were needed when writing comments. The 'reminder prompt' was intended for higher achievers who simply needed nudging to elaborate, extend or solve the 'scaffolded prompt' for those who needed some suggestions and the 'example prompt' for students who needed improvements explicitly modeled. Interestingly, teachers found that the example prompt mostly led to students making up their own sentence rather than simply copying one of the examples given.

Closing the gap prompts

Reminder prompt	■ How do you think the dog felt here?
Scaffolded prompt	■ Describe the expression on his face. ■ Do you think he was annoyed? How do you think he might have shown this? ■ He was so surprised he . . . . ■ He barked _____ly, running around feeling very _____.
Example prompt	■ Choose one of these or your own: ■ He couldn't believe his eyes! ■ He ran round in circles looking for the rabbit, feeling very confused.

For subjects like mathematics, improvements are more about getting to the answer using the appropriate strategies and/or checking calculations. Dylan Wiliam (2011), in his book 'Embedded Formative Assessment', gives helpful examples of how to give worthwhile written comments for mathematics and science:

Vague	Better	Better still
Add some notes on seed dispersal.	Can you suggest how the plant might disperse its seeds?	Give one advantage and one disadvantage of seed dispersal.
Work on your graphing skills.	Think about the accuracy and neatness of your graphs.	One of the axes of your graph is much better than the other. Which one is it and why is it better?
You need to be clear about the difference between power, energy and force.	Check your glossary for the meaning of power, energy and force and then redraft this sentence correctly.	In two seconds, a machine lifts six meters from the ground, a mass weighing ten kilograms. Describe what is happening using the words energy, force and power.

Improvement suggestions can be anything from adding new words or phrases, changing something, such as punctuation, extending or reshaping. In mathematics it might be redoing with advice along the same lines.

One of the simple strategies which Clarke's learning teams discovered was that the space available for students to make subsequent improvements as a result of either teacher comments or peer discussion made a significant impact on the scope of students' improvements. If the left-hand side of exercise books, for instance, are always left blank, this provides a perfect space for both comments by teacher and for later improvements to be made, alongside their original attempts. Where students had been asked to make improvements at the end of their piece, this led to mostly minimum effort.

The following piece (Figure 5.8, with originally a blank left hand side), illustrates the scope of improvement and extension to this 'balanced argument' as a result of two succinct improvement suggestions by the teacher – the improvements filling the blank page!

The use of highlighters to indicate success or 'best bits' and places to improve (often two colors), as illustrated in Figure 5.8, is an efficient way of teachers or students indicating success. Some schools ask students to making any improvements with a different colored pen as a way for all parties involved to differentiate between first and second stages of development.

An important point is that 'improvements' are only improvements, especially in any written piece, only *if they actually enhance the original writing*. Getting students to read their work aloud, or muttered to themselves, helps them see whether their improvements make the piece better or, in some cases, worse! Another point to make about student writing is that sometimes improvements slavishly linked to success criteria can backfire. Video evidence captured by Clarke (2009) followed two 9-year-olds deciding how to improve their writing by looking at the list of

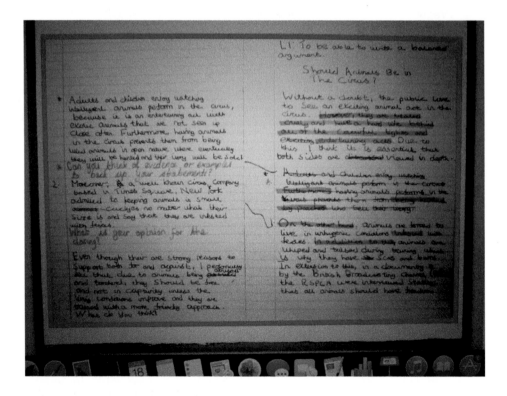

Figure 5.8 Left hand side originally blank for further improvements

'What makes good writing' displayed on the wall. They decided that they didn't have enough similes, and both agreed to think of three each to improve their work. The similes they chose were weak and, rather than enhancing their writing, made it look overwritten and odd, losing its original flow. In trying to think of a good simile to describe a loud noise, for instance, one of the boys settled on 'as loud as a very loud cat'(!). This anecdote is a good illustration of the need to make sure students think about the purpose of the writing, the impact on the reader and which elements of the success criteria will achieve this, and to read their writing aloud to see whether it is enhanced or weakened by the addition of various technical features. It is, of course, students' own reading of a range of texts, and the classroom analysis of excellent examples of writing which, in the end, gives them a sense of what quality in writing looks like, with success criteria creating a supportive framework of compulsory or choice elements.

Checking books for planning purposes

Whether we write comments in students' books or have face to face dialogue, the teacher's job, as frequently stated throughout this book, is the never-ending quest to find out what the students already know, or know at this moment, as a result of what has been taught – and then work with them to move them forward. The responses of the students during a lesson, the work we see in their books as a result and the evidence drawn from lesson starter questions **all combine to guide us in planning the next steps for this learning**. A distinction needs to be made, in order to create the best balance between written comments, oral exchanges and simply checking work, between time spent writing comments in books compared to time saved to plan more efficiently. Sometimes a sampling of students' recent work can make a greater difference to your next lessons than over investment in time reading and commenting on every student's work. At the heart of this balancing act is the importance of knowing the impact of anything we do, and deciding its value based on that knowledge.

Whole class written feedback

Caroline Spalding, a teacher of English in the East Midlands, gave her 16-year-olds the option of individual feedback or class feedback. They voted for the latter, which she presented to them in the following chart (GCSEs are national tests taken at age 16 in the UK), reducing the time she needed to mark all the books and giving them a clear overview of what went well and how they could improve (Figure 5.9). As with all strategies, a balanced approach and deciding which technique will have the best impact for each context is the key to effective but manageable feedback. Caroline explained that the huge GCSE marking workload had been eased by the use of this strategy and codes. Any feedback given is followed up by 'green pen time' throughout the school during which students make improvements.

WHOLE CLASS FEEDBACK – GCSE English Lit Paper 2 'DNA'			

Date: 11/12/16

Spellings 1	Spellings 2	Punctuation and grammar	Vivo Rewards
• characters • cigar**ette** (*ette* = *little*) • euphemism • extr**eme**ly • h**ie**rarchy • play**wright**	• rep**et**ition • sadistic • society • ster**eo**typical • thems**el**ves • vulnerable	• Brian • Don't use inverted commas around character's names or techniques! *It makes you sound sarcastic.* • After a quotation start a new sentence e.g. *This suggests that…*	Charlotte/Jake - quantity Andrew – progress since Y10 Ashley B – exploration of meanings Emma/Ashley T - achievement Annaliese/Lauren – sophisticated ideas *(Monday club!)*

What went well	Even better if
✓ Most people wrote at least two sides of A4 (AO1) ✓ Most people made a range of clearly different points in response to the question (AO1) ✓ Most people made good use of quotations (AO1) – *not just using them, but analysing them in detail (AO2)* ✓ Most people remembered to comment on the playwright's ideas about people/life/society (AO3)	1. You must remember it's a play (not novel) – audience (not reader) and playwright (not writer)! 2. You need to refer explicitly to the context i.e. that this is a modern play and teaching us about modern life 3. Avoid using the word 'quote' 4. You need to link to the whole play; some people are too focussed on just what is happening in their quotations 5. 'Symbolically' refers to all people i.e. the big ideas 6. Remember you don't need to just use one quotation per paragraph. If you can, integrate short quotations throughout your response.

Figure 5.9 Example of whole class feedback

(Caroline Spalding, 2016)

Using marking codes and symbols

A popular strategy to ease the load of marking is the use of codes, letters and numbers linked to English targets, as in the examples below devised by Christopher Curtis (@Xris32) from Saint John Houghton Academy in Ilkeston, and published on his blog. The targets are used in the planning of lessons and the overall sequence of work. They are seen as a starting point, with room for teachers to add more if they want to.

Teachers explain to students the skills needed from the assessment (using the grids) then they teach them. They refer back to the codes throughout the teaching and build lessons around the basic skills. Instead of teachers correcting basic errors, the codes focus on the skills involved and allow for more precision. Using the targets also means that follow up teaching and differentiation is easier to plan. The targets were adapted for younger classes in the school and are discussed and refined by the English department each year.

Because the school's assessments use numbers, the teachers use letters for targets and numbers for achievement – so when marking all that is written is a letter and/ or a number. If the sheets are in students' books, the relevant target can be easily highlighted.

The impact of the codes approach was improved progress in exam results. In comparison to other subjects (not using the targets and codes), English was one of the best performing subjects in the school, in terms of levels of progress.

Travel topic writing (11- to 14-year-olds)

These targets are given to students at the start of this topic for 11–14 year olds. Teachers use them as learning intentions for lessons and refer to them throughout their teaching and in the drafting and marking process.

	Skill
1	Describe a setting in great detail, creating a particular mood or effect.
2	Use facts in writing to develop detail.
3	Use opinions to influence the reader.
4	Use exaggeration for a particular effect – shock, humor.
5	Select words to help create a particular mood.
6	Select less obvious words to describe things.
7	Develop the description by expanding the noun phrases.
8	Use a range of punctuation marks for effect.
9	Use punctuation to help create a specific effect.
10	Vary the tone of your writing to maintain the interest of the reader.
11	Vary the structure and types of sentences used.
12	Use figurative language (similes, metaphors, personification) for effect.
13	Structure and present the text in a creative, imaginative and effective way.
14	Develop a consistent style of writing across the whole text.
15	Create links across the whole text, such as a running theme or joke.

Writing (16-year-olds)

A	Write in clear sentences.
B	Use commas to separate parts of a sentence and for lists.
C	Use punctuation marks correctly (? ! ’).
D	Make sure commonly used words are spelt correctly.
E	Use connectives to link sentences together.
F	Use paragraphs to separate ideas.
G	Make your writing suitable for the audience – formal / informal.
H	Make your writing sound and look like the text is supposed to be.
I	Use a range of sentence openings / lengths for effect.
J	Use a range of punctuation marks for effect.
K	Use a variety of paragraph lengths for effect.
L	Make sure your writing is structured effectively – links / opening / closing.
M	Develop ideas in paragraphs by using counter arguments.
N	Build links across the text.
O	Vary the tone of your writing across the text.
P	Aim for a consistent style of writing across the text.
Q	Use knowledge from other sources within your writing.
R	Use humour (irony, satire or parody).

Reading (16-year-olds)

A	Select quotes from the text to support your ideas.
B	Use speech marks ('quote') to show you have used a quote.
C	Use specific language terms – simile, metaphor, alliteration.
D	Use grammar terms – verbs, nouns, nouns, adverbs, adjectives.
E	Zoom in on specific words or phrases.
F	Use correct words to describe the technique / word used.
G	Explain what the reader is supposed to feel.
H	Explain why the writer chose the technique / word.
I	Explain how this word / technique links to the whole extract.
J	Follow the 'technique and effect' sentence structure.
K	Use a wider range of points – word, phrase, technique and sentence form.
L	Links techniques together with a similar effect or spot patterns.
M	Use a wide number of short quotes in response.
N	Use advanced terminology – passive, sentence, assonance, pathetic fallacy.
O	Explore how there is more than one possible feeling / effect.
P	Comment on how sentences are used for impact.

For all students, but mainly 11- to 14-year-olds, the school uses the following success criteria sheets, with specific examples. These are given to students or students can select to use them.

Improving writing: sentences   Name:

To enhance your learning, you need to:

- Vary how you start your sentences
- Vary the length of your sentences
- Use a variety of sentence structures

Rewrite a paragraph in your writing and try to improve the sentences.

- Make sure they all start with a different word
- Use a question or command in your sentences
- Make one of your sentences short (1–4 words long)
- Try to start some of your sentences with a verb (running), an adverb (slowly), an abstract noun (fear) or a preposition (under)
- Or try to use some of these sentence structures:

_____ , _____ , _____ .

_____ , _____ .

_____ ? _____ .

Improving writing: punctuation   Name:

To improve your learning, you need to:

- Use all punctuation marks correctly
- Use a variety of punctuation at least once (- : ; ,. ?. . .! ')
- Use some complicated punctuation accurately (:;-)

Rewrite a paragraph in your writing and try to improve the punctuation

- Read the paragraph again and check that no full stops are missing.
- Check that commas have been use correctly. Would it make sense as a sentence on its own? Sometimes we put two sentences together with a comma, when a full stop is just as good.
- Add a bracket, question mark or exclamation mark to your writing. You don't need all of them.
- Find two sentences that are closely linked together and join them together with a semicolon, instead of a full stop.
- A colon (:) introduces a new item. For example -- It was a day I always hated: Monday. Try to use one colon in your writing.

The full list of these includes paragraphs, interesting content, presentation, use of PEE, evidence and deeper meaning. They can be found at: http://learningfrom-mymistakesenglish.blogspot.com (Christopher Curtis, 2016; Twitter @Xris32). Christopher writes, in an explanatory blog, a rationale for the department's method of planning and marking:

I look at exercise books all the time. I scrutinise exercise books as head of the English department. Not because I want to chase people and tell them off for not marking but because I want to see what the learning looks like in that person's lessons. How has the learning been shaped? How has the student developed over time? What has the teacher done with a topic? How have they supported a student? I suppose, if I am honest, I don't look at things the way others look at things: desperate for some evidence of progress or no progress. The things I look at are:

1) What is the learning that has taken place?
2) What activities have students done to enable the learning to take place?
3) How has the teacher's marking guided the student to improve?

So, what did I do with my department about the target setting issue? I extended the bank of targets. I gave them more. I gave them topic related targets. I gave them targets for reading and targets for writing. I even made it easier for teachers by giving a skill a letter or number. The teacher gives the student a number and they copy that skill into their books. We have shared these skill sheets this year and we are going to build on them next year.

We made the skills explicit to students. They knew what the targets were going to be at the start of the topic. In fact, the teaching was planned around the targets we might set the students. Therefore, students were able to see how things linked to the overall task. They self-evaluate the targets throughout a topic.

(Christopher Curtis, 2016)

Not only are teachers relieved of the burden of copious individual book marking, they are also guided by the appropriate learning targets. The specificity of the success criteria is the key to helping students know exactly how to improve. Where examples are given, meanings are even clearer.

Another system for avoiding writing the same thing repeatedly in students' mathematics books and easing the marking workload is to create a symbol for the common errors detected (as in the examples below), simply write those in students' books, then have the symbols and their explanations written or projected on the smart board at the beginning of the next lesson. They copy the written explanation into their books and then follow that advice during improvement making.

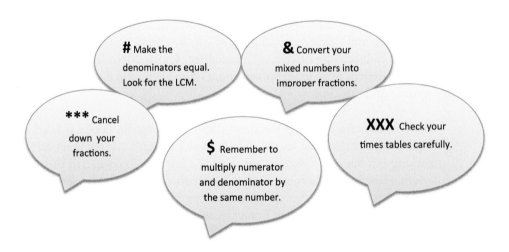

With the number of students, a secondary teacher has to deal with in one day, this seems an excellent strategy for giving personalized written feedback which helps the student to improve, without being, as Dylan Wiliam (2015) puts it '*more work*

for the donor than the recipient'. Any written feedback should rarely be longer than the student's work.

Helen Joannou from Almond Hill School, Stevenage, created a manageable marking system for mathematics with her class. Depending on how each student tackles a task, she assigns their next task as either E for enrichment, R for reinforcement or M for misconception. The students sit next to their random talk partner (changing weekly) so no form of ability grouping exists and students have the opportunity to learn from each other and see the mathematics topic at different levels of complexity. This kind of differentiation, not fixed, and linking with the different 'learning zones' (panic, challenge and comfort zones) helps students feel they are at the right level for them at this moment. One example can be seen below (Figure 5.10), then student comments about the system (Figure 5.11).

In an ideal world, teachers would have 1–1 discussions with students every day, but in reality, a balance has to be struck between detailed written feedback, symbol or short written feedback, whole class feedback based on looking through their work, structured peer feedback and 1–1 discussions when possible.

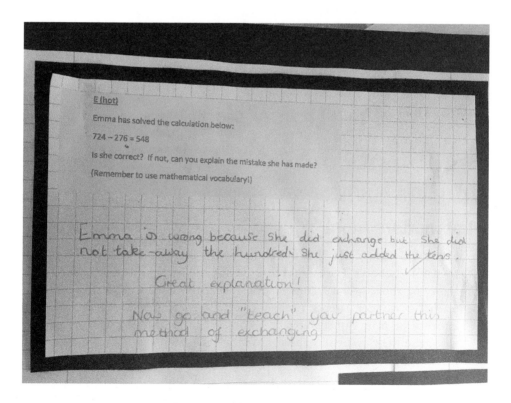

Figure 5.10 Use of follow-up differentiation

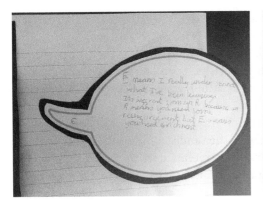
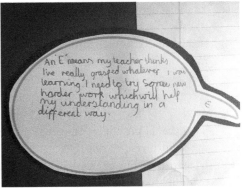
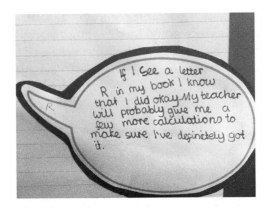

Figure 5.11 Student comments

d) Feedback to and from parents and other school partners

What matters most

Hattie and Peddie (2003) analyzed the reports that had been sent home to parents from 150+ schools. They found that the majority of students in these schools were achieving above average, conscientiously making an effort and were a pleasure to teach. No wonder parents demand more 'tests', accountability, and 'teacher-proof' information from our schools. The most significant feedback we can give parents is to raise their awareness about how they can best help their child's learning at home. That is 'their learning'.

Hong and Ho (2005) found that parent aspirations were the most important influence on their children's achievement (d = 0.80), whereas parental supervision in the forms of monitoring students' homework, time watching screens and time going out with friends appeared to have a negative effect on the educational aspirations of adolescent students (see also Clinton & Hattie, 2013). Also, having a negative effect were external rewards, negative control and restrictions for unsatisfactory grades.

To augment these findings, schools need to work in partnership with parents and other care givers to make their expectations appropriately challenging and clear:

> Parents should be educated in the language of schooling, so that the home and school can share in the expectations, and the child does not have to live in two worlds – with little understanding between the two.
>
> *(Hattie, 2009)*

Teachers, via their students, could share the learning intentions and success criteria to inform parents of the current focus of learning. Also, there are now some great apps where teachers can take a pause during the day and ask students to use the app to comment on their learning – which is sent to parents so that this could be a focus of discussion at home. Rather than asking 'What did you DO today at school?', the discussion can be 'Tell me about what you learnt, discovered or got helpful feedback about today'.

This is not the book to delve into homework other than to say: ensure the homework, where it exists, is more related to an opportunity to practice something already taught in school, otherwise students with parents who cannot or are disinclined to help their children are penalized. Of course, there are also occasions where the student might not have understood the lesson to which the homework is related, which can cause similar problems. Homework is school work done at home and needs teacher feedback on this work, to make the message clear and to show that this work is part of school learning.

Use of video as feedback to parents

Although time consuming, in some instances, the use of video can communicate so much more than our words, whether oral or written. Alison Peacock, in her book 'Assessment without limits', cites a teacher, Sharon Peckham, from Meredith School in Portsmouth, who used video to communicate to a parent about his 5-year-old daughter's English language development:

> Having arrived with no English, by the end of the first term Leva was communicating in English with her friends. By the spring she was fluent. Leva's father, not having a great deal of English, asked on parents' evening whether Leva was happy. He believed her English to be poor so worried that she hadn't made friends. Sharon played the video footage to the father of Leva in conversation with her friends. There Dad sat, eyes filled with tears, face filled with love and pride, as he watched his daughter chat away. Sharon realized that this video clip had given Leva's father so much understanding about his daughter and her

achievements. It transpired that Leva never spoke English at home so this was the first time Leva's father had listened to her speaking English. The video was later shared with Leva's grandparents who lived abroad.

(Peacock, 2016)

Although the video footage described demonstrated the achievement of Leva, it is likely that it did far more than that. The father now has a better understanding of his daughter so will probably behave differently with her and her teachers. It is possible that this one video episode could impact everything that happens in the home from now on, with the father now having peace of mind about his daughter and new respect for her abilities.

Student-led learning review meetings

Alison Peacock has become well known for the learning review meetings she established in her school, The Wroxham School in Potter's Bar. These are entirely led by 10- and 11-year-old students, examples of which can be found on YouTube. The following is a synopsis of how this has been achieved, taken from Alison's book:

Learning review meetings at Wroxham are held twice a year. The meetings last for 15 minutes and are held in the school leader's office. Each student presents a set of slides illustrating their self-assessed views of their successes and challenges across the curriculum. The presentation is prepared independently by each student in lessons in the previous week and serves as a structure for dialogue between the student, her teacher, her parents and the school leader. During the meeting, as the student presents, discussion ensues about how to support her in her learning the next steps to achieve further progress. The student or teacher might refer to work within her books to illustrate a point of discussion, thereby providing the parents with detailed insight into ways they might be able to support the student's learning.

As school leader I attend all meetings . . . I gain insight into the student's self-review, the quality of her work, her relationship with her teachers and the support her family are able to offer. This provides a rigorous framework for formative assessment for all concerned. The essential message and importance of learning review meetings is that it is the student herself who is the most important participant.

Other schools have adopted this format. Kate Richardson, from Greenfield Academy in Bristol, decided to trial the meetings. When she first arrived at the school she had asked students to talk about their learning and found they were unable to answer. By the summer term, having removed ability groups, the students were able to talk about how they learnt best.

> Mark Carlyle, school leader of Scole School, also trialled learning review meetings with our format. He felt 'surprised and impressed' by the way the students presented their PowerPoint presentation to their parents. During the meetings, he jotted down notes of any agreed actions and, by taking a back step, was able to see how capable the students were of taking the lead and behaving as the expert. On several occasions he found that students' confident self-reflections exceeded his preconceived views of what they might say.
>
> The commitment to learning review meetings usually amounts to two full days and two evenings in the autumn and spring terms, with some additional meetings for those who cannot make the days. School leaders carrying out this role over time are able to build a rigorous picture of each individual student's strengths and learning needs while also supporting quality of teaching and professional learning in an enabling way.
>
> *(Peacock, 2016)*

When one compares the hours commonly spent on recording 'evidence' of student achievement or learning needs to ensure that no student 'falls through the net', it seems sometimes that we might have missed the point, and that a few deeply meaningful meetings, as described above, can be more effective in enabling all parties involved in the learning of a student to be fully engaged and aware of learning needs, no-one more than the student his or herself.

A key consideration before deciding to run student led feedback sessions is to ensure that this is common in every class and in the culture of the school, with clear expectations. Otherwise, the one-off student–parent event will take too much practice and preparation time and become a burden for teacher and student alike. It should become common practice for students to know about their learning, how close they are to the success criteria of every task and be keen to seek feedback about how to improve or where to next. This is the epitome of great learners, as then they become their own teachers.

Written reports to parents

The format for written reports to parents is very familiar to most teachers, with some kind of description against some kind of criteria, whether school, district or national. As we noted above, students are performing well, putting in effort and are a pleasure to teach. Such lies might be 'nice' and lead to good public relations, but make it hard to justify the amount of time that goes into written reports if this is the outcome. Moreover, the norm has been that these are written by teachers and sent to parents, with no input from the student. If we are serious about the student's involvement in their own learning, then it seems important that this involvement is a reality at all stages, from lesson learning to reporting. In Langford School, Fulham, students proofread end of year reports and write their own comment in

Child comment:

I have enjoyed reading my report and I feel happy with the comments.
In Team 2 I have particularly enjoyed History and I can remember lots of interesting facts!
I will work on my times tables in Team 3 and I am looking forward to meeting Ms Are.
Abdullahi

Headteacher comment: What a super report! You should be very proud of your achievements. Well

done!

Signed: Mr. Gibbons

        Headteacher   Class teacher: **Mrs Pickles**

Figure 5.12 Child comment on school report

a provided space. If they are unhappy with what has been written or they would like to question the teacher, they have opportunities to include these comments in the report. It certainly leads to students having more ownership of the reports and their learning. Figure 5.12 is an example from a student's report at the end of the infant years.

Finding opportunities for parents to give feedback

Most schools have parent questionnaires which provide date about parent satisfaction with the school and their child's progress. Parent evenings in which school policy is explained are also common practices. Email exchanges are also common between parents and teachers in many schools.

Hawthornden School in Midlothian decided to provide open afternoons built into the school calendar for what they call 'PATPAL' (pupils as teachers/parents as learners in which children taught their parents something they were learning in their classroom), thus providing perhaps a more informal way of parents being able to see not just what but how their child is learning.

Tracy Jones, school leader from Merllyn School, introduced learner led conferences instead of parent open evenings, as parents tended to be more interested in behavior and compliance than learning. In the learner led conferences, the student presents their learning and they talk about where they are, how they are progressing and their next steps. This has had a positive impact on the conversations the parents have with the teachers about learning.

The schools also introduced a graffiti board for feedback and feedforward, and the children are encouraged to take their parents to write things on the board. Parents asked for more sports (so the school employed a sports apprentice) and improved communication.

The most recent learner led sessions at the school focused specifically on homework. It was interesting that the parents of younger children liked project work and getting involved, but as they got older enthusiasm waned. As a consequence, the staff has reviewed the homework policy to focus on skills – only after students' first year of school (5/6-year-olds). Parent comments can be seen at Figures 5.13 and 5.14.

Parent feedback

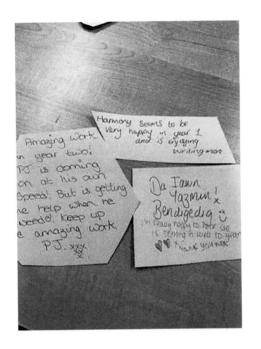
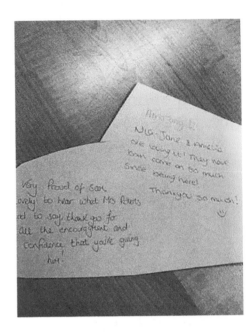
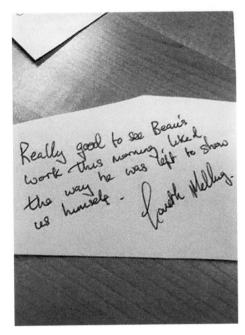
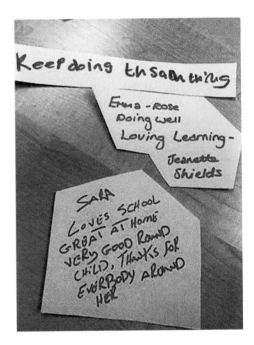

Figure 5.13 The homework focus graffiti board 2017

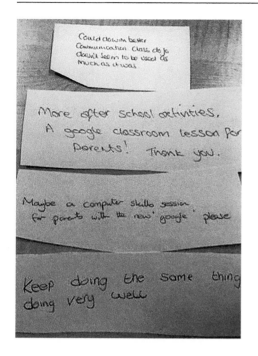

Figure 5.13 (*Continued*)

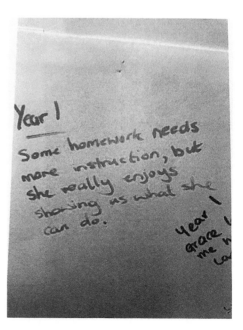

Figure 5.14 Parent comment board (*continued overleaf*)

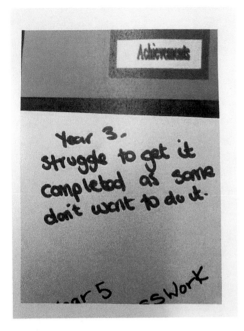

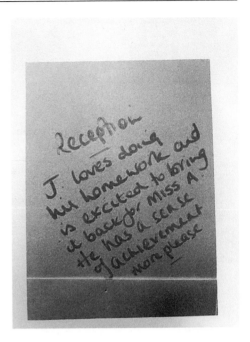

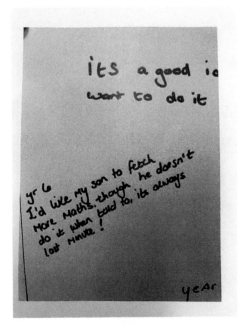

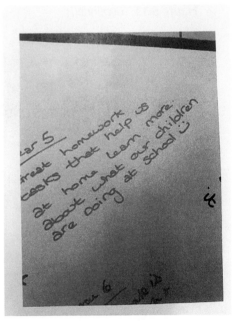

Figure 5.14 (*Continued*)

Flaxmere schools

The schools in Flaxmere are located in the lowest socio-economic parts of New Zealand. They conducted many initiatives to improve the school-home partnership. One was putting computers in the homes, and then hiring ex-teachers to show parents how to use them to help their children's learning. The (initially unanticipated) consequence was that these parents learnt how to trust and learn the language of teachers – and this increased the number of parents who had confidence to go to the school and interact with teachers (Clinton & Hattie, 2013). There are many ways in which we can encourage parents to come to schools to hear the feedback from teachers, and for teachers then to be more confident that their information about students has been heard, interpreted correctly and enacted in the partnership within the home.

Conclusion

There have been two running themes throughout the last two chapters: the evidence that within-lesson feedback (of high quality) is more effective for learning than post-lesson feedback (of low quality), and, where post-lesson feedback exists, it should not merely be for accountability reasons, but should optimally take place if there is improved student progress as a result and the work is manageable for teachers. We would rather see teachers using their time to reflect and plan than be overburdened with often pointless marking of books for marking's and compliance's sake. Remember, marking may not involve feedback.

e) Examples of feedback policies and related thinking by practicing school leaders

The 'politics of distraction'

One of the great disadvantages of an inspection service and/or public comparisons of schools' results, in any country, is that it can encourage schools to engage in practices which they would otherwise not deem useful to student learning. For example, one inspectorate group demanded to see comments on students' books. This led to teachers making students' books look heavily marked and commented upon: adding to teachers' workload and stopping them directing their energies into planning based on the feedback they received in today's lessons. The students have been the losers in this policy.

Fear in a profession, caused by high stakes for the school, leads inevitably to not only teaching to the test, but also unmanageable workload in the continual struggle to prove that teachers are doing their job. The focus then turns to the teacher, not the impact of the teacher on the student. As Charlie Stripp, Director of the UK National Centre for Excellence in the Teaching of Mathematics, said, '*Marking*

FEEDBACK AT LANGFORD PRIMARY SCHOOL

The Sutton Trust EEF toolkit identifies feedback as one of the most powerful tools a teacher has, with research suggesting it can add +8months to a child's learning.

Clear MODELS OF *'EXCELLENCE'* **are shown to learners; left on display and referenced when providing feedback.**

CO-OPERATIVE IMPROVEMENT (CI) **should be used when needed.**

Both pupils focus on 1 book at a time.

The author always holds the purple pen and is allowed to disagree with the feedback.

Visualiser Stops (VS) **are used when needed and a child's learning is chosen at random to be discussed against the WMG.**

IN THE MOMENT FEEDBACK **is recognised as most powerful. VF in books indicates a learning dialogue has happened** .

Ks2 pupils can request feedback **from their teacher in** purple pen **at the end of a lesson.**

EFFECTIVE Feedback

CLOSED LI's **which have been achieved are** highlighted in pink. **No need to tick everything or correct careless errors**

The WMG **in a** closed learning intention **should start with:** 'Remember to...'

CLOSED LI's **which are not fully achieved are left blank with** green feedback **(if it will make a difference!) and highlighted in pink when achieved.**

OPEN LI's **will have best bits in** PINK **and improvements in** GREEN.

The WMG **in an** open learning intention **should start with:** 'Choose from...'

Pupils are ALLOWED TIME **to respond to feedback.**

Teachers: If it won't make a difference...don't do it!

Figure 5.15 Langford feedback policy

should not be about providing evidence that you are doing your job. If that's why you're doing it, you are not doing your job'.

Our purpose for this book is to equip teachers and schools with a foundation of evidence to back up a powerful repertoire of tried and tested feedback strategies. Confidence can be established when we feel clear about these things, and when all staff are equally clear, and can justify all their actions using that evidence – and they can then see the impact on the learning lives of their students.

Three innovative feedback policies now follow with commentary by each school's school leader. Langford Primary School, Fulham, has, unusually, a one-page policy for feedback (see Figure 5.15), encapsulating what matters (WMG – what makes good – or their term for success criteria). All three schools are committed to an emphasis on 'in the moment' feedback and a focus on purpose and impact and are schools with outstanding student achievement as well as staff well-being.

The school leader, Seamus Gibbons, explained their policy:

We believe it is important for students to have all their learning acknowledged. We use the learning intention to support feedback provided to students at Langford. If the learning intention is closed and the student has achieved this, it is simply highlighted in pink. This allows the student to know that they have been successful.

If the learning intention is closed and the student has not achieved it, the teacher will only provide a feedback comment if they feel it will have an impact on the learning. If the student responds to the question correctly, the learning intention is highlighted in pink. Professional judgment is used here. If the teacher doesn't feel the written comment will have impact, it is left and feedback is given either verbally or through whole class teaching.

If the learning intention/learning task is open the teacher will provide feedback about successes and how it could be improved.

One of our core beliefs is that feedback is most effective when sought. Therefore, we allow opportunities for students to request feedback from teachers. Teachers during lessons will ask students what they would like feedback on, but there is also dedicated time that the students reflect on their learning and request feedback from their teacher. This is proving extremely effective, as nearly always we can see that the feedback sought has been used effectively in the final draft of writing.

An example of an open learning intention in English and feedback sought and acted upon:

One student wrote 'Could I have added more to the conclusion?' to which the teacher wrote back 'Explain why and how the drums will motivate you as it isn't that clear'.

The student continued the conclusion . . .

And to always listen to the drums to motivate you if the game goes on for days, as the beat and rhythm will keep you playing.

Excerpt from the student's final draft:

10) Following on, someone from the losing team shall need to be sacrificed. This shall probably be the captain. Now you know about this inspiring game, you can free yourself and your friends from boredom. Also, I strongly advise you not to play if you don't have protective padding and to always listen to the drums to motivate you if the game goes on for days, as the beat and rhythm will keep you playing.

(Omar M.)

Flora Barton, school leader of Crowmarsh Gifford School, writes the following in her blog 'Headsmart . . . reflections of a head teacher'. Not only is the feedback policy emphasizing the 'in the moment' feedback but she encourages a healthy work/life balance, an essential component of retaining staff with energy and a sense of being truly valued.

Reflections of a head teacher

The key thing to think about is 'What is the purpose of what we are doing?' In fact, we use this question constantly to fully evaluate what we do, why we do it and what impact it is truly having. It means we often change the 'status quo' because we want to do what's best for our students and our school. Key to any policy change is also to think about the impact of what we are doing to support teacher workload.

The reason I expect staff to leave twice a week by 4.15, is because as a school we put in processes and policies specifically to help ease the workload. I do expect staff to look after their wellbeing, and having time to enjoy our life outside of school makes us more effective in our roles. I cover classes to give teachers time, and gain great insight into every child: I cover teachers marking national tests, I give each teacher a day to write their reports and even offer a 'duvet' day in the summer for them to use as they like.

Feedback within the classroom is just one huge aspect of helping teachers' workload. In fact, one of our senior teachers is now coming to the full second year of not having taken a book home to mark – but the impact on student progress has been phenomenal. For a week, I sat and interviewed every student in that class, to have them 'prove' their learning to me. They talked through every book, explaining the feedback and their next steps and how they are applying the feedback to their learning. There are now many examples, across the entire school, of this increased level of student achievement.

All of this does come with a note of caution – you can't just jump on the newest craze and expect it to work in your school, unless the conditions are right. We are coming to our second year of verbal/in the moment feedback and it has taken this time for all teachers to begin to embed it in daily practice. Transformational change takes time. Questioning the 'status quo' is central to this, so we research everything before we adopt it across the school. We test things in class, talk to the children, establish what works and what doesn't. This is the key – looking for what has greatest impact while questioning its purpose.

Teachers are what make our schools amazing – we have to do what we can to look after them, so that every day they come into school with passion, energy and enthusiasm to bring learning to life for every child in their classroom. If you are a school leader, I would seriously consider what processes you have in place to help support your team. Ask them what would help and see what you could feasibly offer. Taking care of your staff means that you are taking care of your students – it will help transform the culture of your school.

Feedback policy: Crowmarsh Gifford CE Primary School

The major message seems to be that students – regardless of achievement level – prefer teachers to provide more feedback that is forward looking, related to the success of the lesson, and 'just in time' and 'just for me', 'about my work' (and not about me).

It is not sufficient simply to tell a student where they have gone wrong – misconceptions need to be explained and improvements for future work suggested.

The mistake I made was seeing feedback as something teachers provided to students. I discovered that feedback is most powerful when it is from the student to the teacher. What they know, what they understand, where they make errors, when they have misconceptions, when they are not engaged – then teaching and learning can be synchronized and powerful. Feedback to teachers makes learning visible.

(Hattie, 2012)

Purpose of feedback

In constructing this policy staff have considered the following factors:

- Why has work been marked?
- Who is it for?

- Can the child access the feedback given?
- How does it promote learning?
- Has it been effective?
- Have children responded appropriately?
- Is this marking necessary?

Key to feedback

As Sadler (1989) states, children must be clear about what they are doing well now, where they are aiming to get to and, more crucially, how they close the gap between the two (Black and Wiliam 1998b).

When scrutinizing feedback in school, it has been apparent that teachers might mark because they feel it is expected by school inspectors, parents or senior leaders in school. This is not the case. We know from research and experience, that marking can consume most of a teacher's time outside of lessons, therefore we have given a high priority to workload considerations when drafting this policy. When thinking about feedback and marking, if it is not useful for the students themselves, or for the teacher, then there is no reason to do it – we would question its purpose.

Why is feedback so important in our school?

- It gives meaningful feedback to the child
- When done correctly maximizes learning potential
- Child is at the center of the learning
- Helps children learn how to be the best learners they can be
- Informs planning by highlighting areas for development, enabling the child to make clear improvements
- Is integral to the planning of future lessons and informs progress assessments
- Facilitates and improves communication between learners, teachers and teaching assistants

What should feedback look like in the classroom?

- Dialogue – everyone talking about their learning and next step improvements
- Learning continually being evaluated and adapted
- Ongoing observations of children
- Children clear about where they are now, where they need to get to and most crucially, how to close the gap between the two
- Children as active learners

- Questioning between students and adults
- Regular learning conversations within lesson with individuals, groups and whole class
- Children developing an understanding of what quality learning looks like
- Ongoing modeling or and coaching in self and peer assessment

Methods of feedback

Verbal with written

Through observation, class discussions and student interviews, it has been established that verbal feedback is the most effective form of feedback in helping the child to understand where they have succeeded and what they must do to improve.

The quality of the feedback is crucial: using higher order questioning, modeling and exemplification should not be reserved until the completion of a piece of work. Indeed, such feedback given whilst the work is ongoing enables the child to immediately experiment with, develop and implement the new items.

> *Students find teachers' feedback confusing, non-reasoned and not understandable. Worse, students often think that they have understood the teacher's feedback when they have not, and even when they do understand, claim to have difficulties in applying it to their learning'*
>
> *(Goldstein, 2006; Nuthall, 2007 in Hattie, 2012)*

Verbal

We do not require teachers to write 'VF' in books where verbal, on the hoof feedback has been given, but students should be able to articulate how they can improve that piece of learning or apply it to another piece.

Written marking notes

This should be used with caution. We have discussed the use of praise within this and ensuring we only praise effort when it is linked to achievement. Where written feedback is used, it should be recorded in a manner suited to the attainment level of the child to ensure they have full comprehension of its meaning. Time must always be factored into a lesson for the child to read and respond to the comments – if comments are not read by the child, there is no purpose for them at all, unless they are intended for another adult who would find them useful. NOTE: if followed by verbal feedback and explanation, its benefit can be enhanced.

Child-led feedback

The following forms of child-led feedback are vital. In every class, however, these types of feedback must be explicitly taught, reviewed and become an integral part of the learning process.

Self-marking

Completed within lessons, self-marking provides children with immediate feedback enabling them to correct work, check methodology, seek advice or support and make improvements while the objective and process are most relevant. We encourage daily mathematics self-marking to take place, giving the teacher time to use this feedback to plan the following lesson effectively.

Marking their own work allows time to reflect upon their progress towards achieving personal targets helping them to take control of their learning. For effective self-review to take place, they should review their work against success criteria. This also gives an opportunity to reflect on their learning, thinking through the learning traits that were necessary.

Peer feedback

Provides opportunities for children to write for a different audience, consider their own targets in more detail, develop the language of learning required to progress in their own targets and to see the work of others, exposing them to exemplification of higher standards of work.

> *Students and peers regarded giving and receiving feedback to be a potentially enriching experience because it allowed them to identify their learning aps, collaborate on error detection, develop their ability to self-regulate, including monitoring their own mistakes, and initiate their own corrective measures or strategies. A major message is that the positive value of peer feedback requires deliberate instructional support (such as the use of Gan's model) of the three major feedback levels and associated prompts for each level.*
>
> *(Hattie, 2012)*

Purple pens

Where appropriate, children respond to all types of feedback by improving their work, indicated by use of the 'purple pen'. They are also encouraged to use a purple pen to edit their work, to highlight the importance of the processes involved.

Ongoing research

We are continuing to experiment with different ways of improving the effectiveness of feedback. In particular, methods are being explored, analyzed and developed to maximize opportunities for different types of verbal, in the moment feedback within each lesson and to ensure it is factored into weekly plans as an integral part of teaching and learning.

Focusing on oral feedback and formative assessment: one school's revolution

Jeremy Hannay, the school leader of Three Bridges Primary School, in Southall, an award winning school, wrote a much-read article in a leading resource for teachers, *Teach Primary*, in which he described how his school 'wiped the slate clean' from copious written accountability marking as feedback to a more effective approach. The article is reproduced here, as it will resonate with many schools across the world and perhaps inspire confidence to break away from ineffective approaches to feedback, which focus more on accountability than student learning. The school's feedback policy follows . . .

Feedback myths

Coming from Ontario, Canada, I was immediately shocked by the inordinate amount of marking that was taking place here in the UK. When I asked why everyone was spending so much time putting comments in books I was greeted with a range of answers. 'That's the policy here', 'How else will they know what to fix or how to improve?', 'We need evidence in the books', 'It's what we do' and 'I have no idea'. Once in a while I would also hear something like 'It's what research says is best practice'. When people mention this 'research' often they are referring to one of two documents: *the Teaching and Learning Toolkit, originally commissioned by the Sutton Trust, and John Hattie's 'Visible Learning'*, which places feedback in the top five teaching influences on student achievement. Neither publication, however, suggests that written feedback is crucial. In fact, in both reports, specific mention is given to other modalities (student to teacher feedback or metacognitive strategies such as Assessment for Learning).

Cut it out

At my school, we have drastically reduced the amount of written feedback we expect of our teachers. Feedback all told, however, is sharply on the rise (over 20 per cent). More importantly, the decrease in the marking and extensive proforma, based planning we do has been mirrored by an increase in attainment.

So what does our approach include? We've developed an ethos in which teachers can focus on both their own professional learning and that of the students. We've created an environment where teachers can spend their working time developing technological strategies and pedagogical practices that promote student to student feedback. We introduced approaches that foster targeted talk about process and that promote self-regulation. And we encourage students to think about where they are going, how well they are getting on and what's next.

Having read a review of international research and practice, we decided that oral formative feedback and questioning would form the basis for our pedagogical advancements and teaching and learning strategy . . .

In our English program, we've combined 'Talk for Writing' (Pie Corbett) – which involves students learning extensively about a genre of writing in order to increase their capacity to self-reflect, co-construct and feedback on their own and each other's work – with Transactional Strategies instruction (a reading comprehension approach). Teachers share the responsibility of conducting a thoughtful discussion about a common text with students, who are also expected to explain their use of strategies and to communicate reflective responses to what they have read.

In mathematics, our adopted approach is similar to the Singaporean style, and includes thoughtful questioning of the students by the teacher, of the teacher by the students and the students of each other. The feedback and questioning are based on quality first methods, framed using formative assessment and lots of talk about process, encouraging high levels of self-regulation.

Last year we introduced iPads and focused on the use of 'animated thinking'. The students are able to explain themselves through video, voice over animation and photography. It allows them to access the feedback of the teacher and other experts, including classmates, at their own pace. This means every child can confidently integrate technology into his or her learning in a meaningful and engaging way. When the feedback is visible it is exceptional.

In addition to program and pedagogical changes, we also support the use of oral formative feedback strategies and targeted questioning, embedded across the curriculum, such as these:

Constructive feedback

Students of all ages are explicitly taught to use language frames to interact with one another (e.g. 'I can see what you're thinking, but may I challenge you to think . . .?')

Shared ownership

In mathematics lessons, a problem is posed by the teacher and students discuss this with one another as the teacher facilitates the discourse, moving the thinking and questioning from one student to the next, periodically dropping in a new line of thinking.

Two-minute meetings

Each week these are used to confer with students and are often led by questions about learning. 'Tell me about how well you're getting on with . . .', 'Show me an example of . . .' and so on. They are focused conversations using meaningful and specific talk about improvement. The capstone of this process is a termly meeting between the student and teacher, followed by a meeting between the student, teacher and parent to discuss progress and next steps.

(Jeremy Hannay, Three Bridges Primary
in Southall, London)

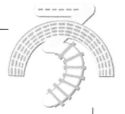

Three Bridges Primary School
Building bridges for a better future

Feedback policy

What is feedback?

We acknowledge that feedback comes in a variety of forms and should be a regular and robust part of every lesson. Feedback, as in integral part of the learning process, must be precisely positioned and delivered regularly in each aspect of the lesson. All feedback should have a positive tone. It should be specific, clear and appropriate in its purpose and productive in its outcomes. The best feedback, whether it is written or verbal, will give students a clear sense of how they can improve, with students responding and making progress as a result.

Aims of feedback @ Three Bridges

   I. To help students make progress.
   II. To provide strategies for students to improve.
  III. To give students dedicated time to reflect upon their learning and put effort in to make improvements.
  IV. To inform planning and structure the next phase of learning.
   V. To facilitate effective and realistic target setting for students and/or the teacher.
  VI. To encourage a dialogue to develop between student and teacher.
 VII. To encourage students to have a sense of pride in their work.
VIII. To encourage students to perfect presentation.
  IX. To correct mistakes with a focus on literacy and mathematics skills and strategies.

Principles of feedback @ Three Bridges

   I. Feedback should be timely and respond to the need of the individual learner so that they can actively engage with the feedback.
  II. A dialogue, both verbal and written, should be created: between the teacher and student, between the students at large, or between the student and themselves. It is essential to allow time for students to engage with feedback and enact that which they feel is relevant and important to moving their learning forward.
 III. Students should be encouraged to assess their own work against collaboratively created learning goals.

IV. Peer and self-feedback are valuable tools for learning that should occur regularly, after careful structuring by the teacher.

Type and frequency of verbal feedback @ Three Bridges

I. This is the most frequent form of feedback.

II. It has immediacy and relevance as it leads to direct student action.

III. Verbal feedback may well be directed to individuals or groups of students; these may or may not be planned for, but will be based on acute and strategic assessment for learning.

Type and frequency of peer feedback @ Three Bridges

I. This is shown by research to be one of the most effective modes of feedback. Effective peer feedback is rigorously structured and modeled by the teacher. These structures are seamless and integrated into the school's pedagogic model.

II. Students need to be well trained over time to effectively peer assess one another. This process will be led by all teachers.

Type and frequency of self-reflection, assessment and feedback @ Three Bridges

I. Akin to peer feedback, students need an explicit and clear structure to identify their learning needs.

II. Teachers should both help uncover and share the elements of success in learning where appropriate.

Formative & oral formative feedback strategies @ Three Bridges

I. In order for a consistent and collective approach to providing strong feedback in lessons, the following list of strategies has been compiled. These strategies form part of the school's pedagogic model and are not 'bolted on' to lessons. Formative and oral formative strategies, such as:

- The ABC Strategy (agree with . . . build upon . . . challenge . . .).
- TPPPTPPP Strategy (teacher, student, student, student, teacher).
- Visible Learning strategies through Explain Everything (iPad provisions – see footnote for explanation of EE).
- Live editing (iPad provision).
- Group Guided or Shared Activities.
- Teacher / Student metacognitive sharing/modelling.
- Think/Pair/Share.
- One-to-one sessions.
- Opinion Lines.

- Enquiry Walls and Post-it Responses.
- Learning Spies.
- Anchor tasks.
- Procedural and Conceptual Variation.

Type and frequency of written feedback @ Three Bridges

I. Written feedback will only be used when the teacher determines that it is the most effective and relevant type of feedback for the subject/lesson/student or context. It will be the least frequently used form of feedback in most contexts.

II. Written feedback will model all aspects of our presentation/handwriting expectations.

III. When determined appropriate to use, written feedback will be a balance of the positive reinforcement of mastered skills and clear, current and actionable ideas to improve their work.

IV. This may include identifying specific issues such as key words, presentation issues, spellings etc. and students should act upon these.

English & mathematics feedback

I. If the English standards of our students are going to improve, we must all give appropriate and targeted feedback. For students to take pride in their work they must realize that spelling, grammar and punctuation are not just important in English lessons but are essential for successful communication everywhere. It should be monitored in all forms of feedback.

II. We all have a duty to be vigilant about standards of our students' mathematics where appropriate. For example, concepts such as graphs, ratio, proportion, etc. should be monitored accurately across the curriculum.

Monitoring and evaluation @ Three Bridges

I. We are all the stewards of every child and ultimately responsible for the highest standards of work from ourselves and our children. Senior Leaders will provide support and development related to feedback as part of every induction process and review and revisit core strategies every year.

II. We, both teachers and senior leaders, share in the expectation and responsibility that all students will progress in their learning. This may involve INSET, informal teacher-initiated conversations or more formal approaches, such as Lesson Study.

III. A range of evidence will be triangulated in partnership between teachers and senior leaders when looking at the quality and impact of feedback at Three Bridges: conversation with students and staff, work celebrations, internal exemplification and moderations, lesson study conclusions etc.

Footnote

At Three Bridges, 'Explain Everything' is a core app that we use as a strategy for providing both instruction and feedback. Within the app itself, teachers design and deliver learning opportunities that are accessed individually, in small groups or as a class (or all 3!). During lessons, students are encouraged to live-record both written and verbal feedback to each other as part of the learning and are provided with opportunities to wirelessly display that thinking to the whole class or a smaller group, allowing all students to reflect on each other's successes and struggles. Teachers have the chance to video record both conversations and live editing with a student or group of students that everyone can see – but, unlike most visualizers, this can be saved and displayed at a later date in a different lesson, replayed as many times as a student would like and at a time that the student finds best for him or her. Students save their work and are able to access it at different points throughout the year to see progress, on top of being able to reflect upon the feedback they have given and enacted over time.

These three policies demonstrate how differently the aims and practice of a school can be presented: one-page summary, research references, numerous different headings. Whatever the style, what matters, of course, is that the policy reflects the reality of the practice in the school, and is continually evaluated for the effectiveness of its impact. All policies shown make explicit reference to the power of 'in the moment' feedback and provide caution about falling into the trap of giving feedback for the wrong reasons.

Key points

- Student should be given every opportunity to give feedback to teachers during, at the end and after lessons about their learning needs.
- Written feedback should only take place if it clearly improves student achievement and should focus on success and specific improvement suggestions for that piece of work.
- Face to face feedback discussions can have more impact than marking.
- Other methods of marking: checking for planning, whole class one sheet feedback, use of marking codes can reduce unmanageable marking workload.
- The politics of distraction (accountability measures) can encourage teachers to focus their efforts too much on outcomes and away from learning.
- Parents and other outside school partners need to be given ways of giving and receiving feedback to and from the school.
- Student-led review meetings can be more effective than traditional parent teacher meetings.
- Written reports to parents can profit from student involvement in writing them.

Final words

The main aim of this book is to resolve the paradox – why is feedback so powerful and why is it so variable? The resolution is knowing about the most effective forms of feedback to give at the optimal phase of learning, to frame the feedback to the three major feedback questions and to emphasize the 'Where to next/how to improve' feedback'. We have also highlighted the importance of teachers' modeling, receiving, interpreting and remodeling their teaching in light of the feedback they receive about the impact of their teaching. Teachers who react to feedback about their teaching show the students the power of feedback. They show they have listened, and thus changed, modified or re-taught. Finally, we aimed to show that errors, not knowing and misconceptions are opportunities for learning and are the occasions when the power of growth mindset thinking is most needed.

We started this book noting the power of feedback, but also noted the seeming paradox that not all feedback is powerful; even the same feedback in different situations. Our aim throughout this book is to unravel this paradox. By now, we hope you see the major issues – the power of feedback depends on the receiving skills of the learner as much as the feedback messages provided by the giver; it depends on the phase of learning (surface too deep to transfer) as to its value to be received and inform the next phases of learning; and critically, it depends on whether the received not only hears and understands the feedback but also whether they can use it to advance their learning. Hence, we need to focus more on the receiving, the skill, will and motivation of the learner when interpreting the feedback, and as much as possible include feedback that helps the learner move forward.

Key points relevant to reducing the variability and thus maximizing the impact of feedback:

- feedback needs to be focused on whether the learner is at surface, deep or transfer,

- grades or comments with no focus on improvement might interfere with learning,
- comments need to focus on success and improvement.

Dispositions of the learner

The dispositions of the learner are paramount in the worthwhileness of feedback. So often the learner's emotions diffuse the effects of the feedback provided. It is their thoughts, feelings and interpretations that filter the messages. Furthermore, feedback costs – as often it requires reinvestment, re-learning and reinterpretation, which is why so much feedback is not heard, is resisted or denied. Students, too often from an early age in their schooling, learn responses to feedback that can neutralize, mask or misinterpret the incoming feedback, such as only hearing the positive or self-enhancing feedback, failing to listen to the negative information, accepting the positive and scrutinizing the negative narrowly, attributing the positive to self and the negative to anything else, misremembering feedback, and creating self-fulfilling prophecies (Dunning, 2005).

Key points relevant to reducing the variability and thus maximizing the impact of feedback:

- The skill, will and thrill: effective learning and therefore effective feedback needs the skills students bring to the task, the understanding and ability to apply learning dispositions to it, and excitement and curiosity in learning.
- High self-efficacy and trust are needed for feedback to be effective.
- Mindsets and mindframes: we aim for students to think with growth not fixed mindsets when they are challenged or do not know what to do next. Such mindframes involve them knowing how to learn, how to speak about learning, feeling responsible for enhancing their learning and collaborating with others in this learning.
- Errors are opportunities for learning and should not be treated as something to be avoided or signs of failure.
- While praise can help create trust and positive relationships, do not mix praise with feedback about the learning. Praise can detract from investment in learning.
- There is a negative correlation between external rewards and task performance. Feedback in all forms should avoid comparisons with other students.

What students bring to lessons

It is diagnosing what the students bring to the lessons, working with them to show them the criteria for success for the lesson and then conceiving feedback as closing this gap between where they are and where they are desired to be. It is continually getting students to see where they are on the journey towards these appropriately challenging goals. It is a bit like Google Maps – we know where we are going, but there may be many ways to get there, especially if members of the class start from different beginnings. It is the continual, just-in-time, 'where to next' feedback that students thrive on in this learning journey.

> # Key points relevant to reducing the variability and thus maximizing the impact of feedback:
>
> - Prior knowledge is the starting point for feedback.
> - Prior knowledge discussion questions give feedback to teachers which confirm or disconfirm plans for that lesson, thus allowing adjustment.
> - Goals should be specific and challenging but task complexity low.
> - Learning intentions must be known to students, but not necessarily at the start of a lesson. They should be authentic, clear and decontextualized, so that skills can be transferred to other contexts and subjects.
> - Success criteria need to be co-constructed to maximize their impact. They are either compulsory elements in the case of closed learning intentions (rules) or choice items when linked with open learning intentions (tools).
> - Feedback is about closing the gap between current and desired learning.

Role of teachers

We also want teachers to model this feedback process, by being active recipients and listeners to feedback about their impact. We want them to build high trust so that errors and misconceptions are welcomed as opportunities for learning, where assessment is considered feedback to the teacher about their impact (with whom, about what, to what magnitude), and 'where to next' is the essence of the formative evaluative process. This means teachers (as well as students) need defensible understandings of the learning process and where in this process the optimal feedback is needed (task/surface, process/deep, self-regulation/transfer).

> # Key points relevant to reducing the variability and thus maximizing the impact of feedback:
>
> - Student to teacher feedback is most important and consists of a) Where am I going? b) How am I going? and c) How can it be improved and where to next?
> - Students should be given every opportunity to give feedback to teachers during, at the end and after lessons about their learning needs.

- Effective feedback occurs when it is received and acted upon.
- Feedback is part of the formative assessment/evaluation framework: learning intentions, co-constructed success criteria, knowing what good examples look like, effective questioning and effective feedback.
- The SOLO taxonomy is useful for understanding students' developing thinking, helping to move + 1 up the taxonomy and for planning, assessment and providing appropriate feedback.
- Don't assume you know what is happening when asking a student about their work – seek feedback from the student about what is happening.

Strategies of students

Finally, the variability of the power of feedback relates to the strategies students are taught to optimize the feedback they are given, so that they can hear, interpret and use the feedback in their learning.

Key points relevant to reducing the variability and thus maximizing the impact of feedback:

- The more meaningful the context the more likely the learning is to be remembered.
- Forgetting helps us remember better when the content is revisited.
- Spaced, not massed learning is more effective.
- Sometimes less feedback is more, to encourage more problem solving and use of 'stuck' strategies.
- Tasks should have a level of 'desirable difficulties' to maximize achievement.
- Searching questioning and listening to paired student discussions reveal student understanding.
- Students should be activated as learning resources for one another.
- Peer coaching needs training and modeling.

When you walk into your classroom tomorrow, ask not 'What am I doing? How do I best teach?', but instead ask, 'How would I seek feedback from my students about my impact?' This begs the moral purpose question about what you mean by impact (look at your learning intentions and success criteria). It begs the following questions: are ALL your students making the necessary improvements from your lessons; is your class a safe and inviting place to come and learn? It begs the magnitude question as to whether the learning from the lessons was sufficient and, finally, asks how you can improve from this feedback in the next lesson.

All good things for students follow.

Appendix: summary graphics

The following adapted graphic summarizes the evidence for the aspects of feedback covered in this book. With thanks to AITSL in Australia.

The characteristics of good feedback

Aspect	More effective feedback	Ineffective feedback
Setting a goal	A specific and challenging goal is set, often with criteria for a high-quality performance on a task. The goal is communicated so that students understand it (e.g. co-constructed success criteria/excellent examples modeled and analyzed). Feedback addresses task goals directly.	Goals are vague or not used. Students do not understand the goals or the success criteria.

Aspect	More effective feedback	Ineffective feedback
Kind of feedback	Feedback draws attention to positive elements of the performance: for example, the details of correct responses. Feedback includes constructive criticism: advice that provokes the student to improve task performance. Feedback refers to changes in performance from previous efforts. Feedback includes an element of self-assessment by students (including peer assessment) as part of the process of encouraging student autonomy and responsibility.	Feedback is focused solely on incorrect responses. Feedback that does not provide information or support to improve performance or understanding. There is a focus on comparisons with other students, or marks and grades. A reliance on extrinsic rewards (stickers, stars). Feedback includes punishment.
Level of feedback	Feedback provides information about a task, how well it was performed and how to do it more effectively. Feedback at the process level: how can the student improve the learning processes needed to understand and perform the task? Feedback at the self-regulation level: how can the student do a better job of planning, monitoring and managing their actions and using strategies in approaching the task? This is also described as 'metacognitive' feedback.	Non-specific feedback is given: e.g. praise or criticism for task performance without detail. Feedback at the self-level: comment on personal qualities of the student, either positive or negative that provides little or no information about processes or performance.

(Adapted from 'Spotlight – Reframing feedback to improve teaching and learning' AITSL, Australian Institute for Teaching and School Leadership)

The following graphic is taken from Michael McDowell's 2019 publication 'Developing student expertise' and summarizes key learning principles that drive developing expertise:

Learning principle	Description
Deliberate practice	Deliberate and continuous practice over time is necessary to develop mastery. As one practices and gains expertise, new strategies are needed to enhance learning at surface, deep and transfer levels.
Prior knowledge	Children understand new things in the context of things they already know. Activating their prior knowledge and providing opportunities beyond what they know is ideal.
Cognitive load	To think well on a concept or topic, factual knowledge must be developed first before complex thinking may emerge.
Social learning	Learning from others is incredibly powerful in enhancing learning. Peers and experts that provide feedback, modeling and direct instruction are invaluable for learning.
Reinvesting in learning	Understanding and developing dispositions for learning enables people to meet short-term/long-term goals which often affect human emotions.

McDowell (Superintendent for the Ross School District, California) also includes in the book '5Cs for developing student expertise', which succinctly summarize the role of the teacher within lessons:

The 5 Cs for developing student expertise

Promoting clarity – students must constantly know where they are going in their learning, where they are in their learning, and what next steps they need to take. Students have a clear sense of varying levels of complexity in core knowledge and skills they are working towards. Teachers use a variety of strategies to ensure learners have the ability to meet such learning requirements.

Levering challenge – student misconceptions, paradoxes and tensions underlying relationships and patterns of ideas, and contextual differences between problems lay at the fore of learning expertise. Teachers use various strategies to activate challenge and support learners in meeting such challenges.

Consistent checking – teachers are constantly checking in on learner progress towards curricular goals as well as a learner's ability to check their own understanding. This checking underpins approaches to intervention.

Cultivating conversation – a plethora of research has articulated the amount of conversation that occurs among students regardless of a teacher's actions. Teachers use a variety of strategies to capitalize on the demands and attractiveness for socialization as well as the research on dialogue as a key factor in developing expertise.

Tackling contextually rich problems – as students move to transfer they are able to address problems across contexts. Teachers support students in seeing similarities and differences between problems.

Bibliography

Ausubel, D.P. (1968). *Educational psychology: A cognitive view.* New York: Holt, Rinehart and Winston.

Baines, E. (2012). 'Grouping students by ability in school', in P. Adey and J. Dillon (Eds.) *Bad education: Debunking myths in education.* Maidenhead: McGraw Hill, Open University Press.

Bandura, A. (1997). *Self-efficacy: The exercise of control.* Macmillan.

Berger, R. (2013). 'Critique and feedback – the story of Austin's butterfly'. *YouTube.*

Biggs, J.B. and Collis, K.E. (1982). *Evaluating the quality of learning: The SOLO taxonomy (structured of the observed learning outcome).* New York: Academic Press.

Bjork, E.L. and Bjork, R.A. (2014). 'Making things hard on yourself, but in a good way: Creating desirable difficulties to enhance learning', in M.A. Gernsbacher and J.R. Pomerantz (Eds.), *Psychology and the real world: Essays illustrating fundamental contributions to society* (2nd. Edn.) New York: Worth, pp. 59–68.

Bjork, R.A. (1994a). 'Institutional impediments to effective training', in D. Druckman and R.A Bjork (Eds.), *Learning, remembering, believing: Enhancing individual and team performance.* Washington, DC: National Academy Press, pp. 295–306.

Bjork, R.A. (1994b). 'Memory and metamemory considerations in the training of human beings', in J. Metcalfe and A.P. Shimamura (Eds.), *Metacognition: Knowing about knowing.* Cambridge, MA: MIT Press, pp. 185–205.

Bjork, R.A. (2011). 'On the symbiosis of learning, remembering and forgetting', in A.S. Benjamin (Ed.), *Successful remembering and successful forgetting: A festschrift in honor of Robert A. Bjork.* London: Psychology Press, pp. 1–22.

Bjork, R.A. and Kroll, J.F. (2015). 'Desirable difficulties in vocabulary learning', *The American Journal of Psychology*, 128(2), p. 241.

Black, P. and Wiliam, D. (1998a) 'Assessment and classroom learning', *Assessment in Education: Principles, Policy and Practice*, 5(1), pp. 7–73.

Black, P. and Wiliam, D. (1998b) *Inside the black box: Raising standards through classroom assessment.* London: King's College London School of Education.

Black, P.J. and Wiliam, D. (2009). Developing the theory of formative assessment. *Educational Assessment, Evaluation and Accountability*, 21*(1)*, pp. 5–31.

Boaler, J. (2008). *The elephant in the classroom: Helping children learn and love maths.* London: Souvenir Press.

Boaler, J. (2016). *Mathematical mindsets: Unleashing students' potential through creative math, inspiring messages and innovative teaching.* San Francisco: John Wiley & Sons.

Bolton, S. and Hattie, J. (2017). 'Cognitive and brain development: Executive function, Piaget, and the prefrontal cortex', *Archives of Psychology*, 1*(3)*.

Brooks, C. (2017). *Coaching teachers in the power of feedback.* University of Queensland, Australia.

Brousseau, G. (1997). *Theory of didactical situations in mathematics: Didactique des mathematiques (1970–1990).* New York, NY: Springer.

Burnett, P.C. and Mandel, V. (2010). 'Praise and feedback in the primary classroom: Teachers' and students' perspectives', *Australian Journal of Educational and Developmental Psychology, 10*, pp. 145–54.

Burris, C., Heubert, J. and Levin, H. (2006). 'Accelerating mathematics achievement using heterogeneous grouping', *American Educational Research Journal*, 43*(1)*, pp. 103–34.

Butler, R. (1988). 'Enhancing and undermining intrinsic motivation: The effects of task-involving and ego-involving evaluation on interest and performance', *British Journal of Educational Psychology*, 58*(1)*, pp. 1–14.

Carless, D. (2006). 'Differing perceptions in the feedback process', *Studies in Higher Education*, 31*(2)*, pp. 219–33.

Chan, C.Y.J. (2006). 'The effects of different evaluative feedback on students' self-efficacy in learning', Unpublished PhD. University of Hong Kong.

Chiu, M.M., Chow, B.W. and Joh, S.W. (2017). 'Streaming, tracking and reading achievement: A multilevel analysis of students in 40 countries', *Journal of Educational Psychology*, 109*(7)*, pp. 915–34.

Clarke, S. (2001). *Unlocking formative assessment.* London, UK: Hodder and Stoughton.

Clarke, S. (2003). *Enriching feedback in the primary classroom.* London, UK: Hodder Murray.

Clarke, S. (2005). *Formative assessment in the secondary classroom.* London, UK: Hodder and Stoughton.

Clarke, S. (2014) *Outstanding formative assessment.* London, UK: Hachette.

Claxton, G. (2002). *Building learning power, TLO Limited.* Bristol.

Clinton, J. and Hattie, J. (2013). 'New Zealand students' perceptions of parental involvement in learning and schooling', *Asia Pacific Journal of Education*, 33*(3)*, pp. 324–37.

Cohen, G.L. and Garcia, J. (2014). 'Educational theory, practice and policy and the wisdom of social psychology', *Policy Insights from the Behavioral and Brain Sciences*, 1*(1)*, pp. 13–20.

Costa, A.L. and Garmston, R. (2017). 'A feedback perspective', in I. Wallace and L. Kirkman (Eds.), *Best of the best: Feedback.* Carmarthen, Wales: Crown House Publishing.

Costa, A.L. and Kallick, B. (Eds.) (2008). *Learning and leading with habits of mind: 16 essential characteristics for success.* Association for Supervision and Curriculum Development, VA.

Crooks, T. (1988). 'The impact of classroom evaluation practices on students', *Review of Educational Research, 58(4),* pp. 438–481.

Crooks, T. (2001). 'The validity of formative assessments', *British Educational Research Association Annual Conference.* University of Leeds, pp. 13–15.

Curtis, C. (2016). www.learningfrommymistakesenglish.blogspot.com

DCSF (2005). *Higher standards, better schools for all,* Govt. White Paper. England: DCSF.

Deci, E.L., Koestner, R. and Ryan, R.M. (1999). 'A meta-analytic review of experiments examining the effects of extrinsic rewards on intrinsic motivation', *Psychological Bulletin, 125(6),* pp. 627–68.

Deci, E.L. and Ryan, R.M. (1985). *Intrinsic motivation and self-determination in human behavior.* New York: Plenum.

Didau, D. (2015). *What if everything you knew about education was wrong?* Carmarthen, Wales: Crown House Publishing.

Dunning, D. (2005). *Self-insight: Roadblocks and detours on the path to knowing thyself.* New York: Pschology Press.

Dweck, C. (1989). 'Motivation', in A. Lesgold and R. Glaser (Eds.), *Foundations for a psychology of education.* Hillsdale, NJ: Erlbaum.

Dweck C.S. (2000). *Self-theories: Their role in motivation, personality and development.* New York: Psychology Press.

Dweck, C. (2006). *Mindset: The new psychology of success.* New York: Random House Incorporated.

Dweck, C. (2015). 'Carol Dweck revisits the growth mindset', *Education Week,* September 22, 2015.

Dweck, C. (2016). 'How praise became a consolation prize', *The Atlantic,* December 2016, accessed May 16, 2018, www.theatlanticcom/education/archive/2016/12/how-praise-became-a-consolation-prize/510845/

Elewar, M.C. and Corno, L. (1985). 'A factorial experiment in teachers' written feedback on student homework: Changing teacher behaviour a little rather than a lot', *Journal of Educational Psychology, 77(2),* pp. 162–73.

Elliott, E. and Dweck, C. (1988). 'Goals: An approach to motivation and achievement', *Journal of Personality and Social Psychology, 54(1),* pp. 5–12.

Ericsson, K.A., Krampe, R.T. and Tesch-Romer, C. (1993). 'The role of deliberate practice in the acquisition of expert performance', *Psychological Review 100(3),* pp. 363–406.

Francis, B.A.L., Hodgen, J., Pepper, D., Taylor, B. and Travers, M.C. (2016). 'Exploring the relative lack of impact of research on "Ability grouping" in England: A discourse analytic account', *Cambridge Journal of Education 47(1),* pp. 1–17.

Frey, N., Hattie, J. and Fisher, D. (2018). *Developing assessment-capable visible learners, grades K-12: Maximizing skill, will, and thrill.* Thousand Oaks, CA: Corwin Press.

Goldstein, L. (2006). 'Feedback and revision in second language writing: Contextual, teacher and student variables' in K. Hyland and F. Hyland (Eds.), *Feedback in second language writing: contexts and issues.* Cambridge: Cambridge University Press, pp. 185–205.

Hannay, J. (2016). How to stop marking taking over your life. www.teachwire.net/news.

Hattie, J. (2009). *Visible learning: A synthesis of over 800 meta-analyses relating to achievement.* Oxford, UK: Routledge.

Hattie, J. (2012). *Visible learning for teachers: Maximizing impact on achievement.* Oxford, UK: Routledge.

Hattie, J. and Timperley, H. (2007). 'The power of feedback', *Review of Educational Research, 77(1)*, pp. 81–112.

Hattie, J., Biggs, J. and Purdie, N. (1996). 'Effects of learning skills interventions on student learning: A meta-analysis', *Review of Educational Research, 66(2)*, pp. 99–136.

Hattie, J.A.C. (1992). Measuring the effects of schooling. *Australian Journal of Education, 36(1)*, pp. 5-13.

Hattie, J.A.C. and Donoghue, G.M. (2016). 'Learning strategies: a synthesis and conceptual model', *NPJ Science of Learning*, 1, www.nature.com/articles/npjscilearn201613.

Hattie, J.A.C. and Peddie, R. (2003). School reports: 'Praising with faint damns'. *Set: Research Information for Teachers*, 3, pp. 4–9.

Hattie. J.A.C. and Zierer, K. (2018). 10 Mindframes for Visible Learning: Teaching for Success. Oxford, UK: Routledge.

Higgins, R., Hartley, P. and Skelton, A. (2002). 'The conscientious consumer: reconsidering the role of assessment feedback in student learning', *Studies in Higher Education, 27(1)*, pp. 53–64.

Hong, S. and Ho, H-Z. (2005). 'Direct and indirect longitudinal effects of parental involvement on student achievement: Second-order latent growth modelling across ethnic groups', *Journal of Educational Psychology, 97(1)*, pp. 32–42.

Horvath, J.C. (2014). 'The neuroscience of PowerPointTM', *Mind, Brain, and Education, 8(3)*, pp. 137–43.

Kamins, M.L. and Dweck, C.S. (1999). 'Person versus process praise and criticism: Implications for contingent self-worth and coping', *Developmental Psychology, 35(3)*, p. 835.

Kluger, A.N. and DeNisi, A. (1996). 'The effects of feedback interventions on performance: A historical review, a meta-analysis, and a preliminary feedback intervention theory', *Psychological Bulletin*, 119(2), p. 254.

Kohn, A. (1994). 'Grading: The issue is not how but why', *Educational Leadership, 52(2)*, pp. 38–41.

Kulhavy, R.W. (1977). 'Feedback in written instruction', *Review of Educational Research, 47(1)*, pp. 211–32.

Lepper, M.R. and Hodell, M. (1989). 'Intrinsic motivation in the classroom', in C. Ames and R. Ames (Eds.), *Research on motivation in the classroom. Vol. 3*, pp. 73–105. San Diego, CA: Academic Press.

Li, S., Zhu, Y. and Ellis, R. (2016). 'The effects of the timing of corrective feedback on the acquisition of a new linguistic structure', *Modern Language Journal, 100*, pp. 276–95.

Lipnevich, A.A. and Smith, J.K. (2008). 'Response to assessment feedback: The effects of grades, praise and sources of information', *ETS Research Report Series, 2008(1)*, pp. i–57.

Lomas, J.D., Koedinger, K., Patel, N., Shodhan, S., Poonwaia, N. and Forizzi, J.L. (2017). 'Is difficulty overrated? The effects of choice, novelty and suspense on intrinsic motivation in educational games', *Proceedings of the 2017 CHI conference on human factors in computing systems*, pp. 1028–39.

Mayer, R.E. and Moreno, R. (1998). 'A split-attention effect in multimedia learning: Evidence for dual processing systems in working memory', *Journal of Educational Psychology, 90(2)*, pp. 312–20.

McDowell, M. (2019). *Developing student expertise.* Thousand Oaks, CA: Corwin Press.

Merrett, F. and Tang, W.M. (1994). 'The attitudes of British primary school students to praise, rewards, punishments and reprimands', *British Journal of Educational Psychology, 64(1)*, pp. 91–103.

Meyer, W.U., Mittag, W. and Engler U. (1986). 'Some effects of praise and blame on perceived ability and affect', *Social Cognition, 4(3)*, pp. 293–308.

Moser, J., Schroder, H.S., Heeter, C., Moran, T.P. and Lee, Y.H. (2011). 'Mind your errors: Evidence for a neural mechanism linking growth mindset to adaptive post error adjustments', *Psychological Science, 22*, pp. 1484–89.

Nottingham J. (2017). *The learning challenge: How to guide your students through the learning pit to achieve deeper understanding.* Thousand Oaks, CA: Corwin.

Nuthall, G.A. (2005). 'The cultural myths and realities of classroom teaching and learning: A personal journey', *Teachers College Record, 107(5)*, pp. 895–934.

Nuthall, G.A. (2007). *The hidden lives of learners.* Wellington, NZ: NZCER Press.

Nuthall, G.A. and Alton-Lee, A.G. (1997). *Understanding learning in the classroom.* Report to the Ministry of Education. Understanding Learning and Teaching Project 3. Wellington: Ministry of Education.

Nystrand, M. (2006). 'Research on the role of classroom discourse as it affects reading comprehension', *Research in the Teaching of English, 40*, pp. 392–412.

Ofsted (1996). *General Report on Schools*, London, UK: Office for Standards in Education, p. 40.

Podsakoff, P.M. and Farh, J.L. (1989). 'Effects of feedback sign and credibility on goal setting and task performance', *Organizational Behavior and Human Decision Processes, 44(1)*, pp. 45–67.

Peacock, A. (2016). *Assessment for learning without limits*, London, UK: Open University Press.

Pulfrey, C. Buchs, C. and Butera, F. (2011). 'Why grades engender performance – avoidance goals: The mediating role of autonomous motivation'. *Journal of Educational Psychology, 103(3)*, pp. 683–700.

Ramaprasad, A. (1983). 'On the definition of feedback. *Behavioral Science, 28(1)*, pp. 4–13.

Rosenthal, R. and Jacobson, L. (1968). *Pygmalion in the classroom: Teacher expectation and students' intellectual development*. New York: Holt, Rinehart, and Winston.

Rubie-Davies, C. (2017). *Teacher expectations in education*. Oxford, UK: Routledge.

Ryan, A.M. and Shim, S.S. (2012). 'Changes in help seeking from peers during early adolescence: Associations with changes in achievement and perceptions of teachers', *Journal of Educational Psychology*, 104*(4)*, pp. 1122–34.

Ryan, R.M., Miniis, V. and Koestner, R. (1983). 'Relation of reward contingency and interpersonal context to intrinsic motivation: A review and test using cognitive evaluation theory', *Journal of Personality and Social Psychology*, *45*, pp. 736–50.

Sadler, R. (1989). 'Formative assessment and the design of instructional systems', *Instructional Science*, *18*, pp. 119–44.

Santagata, R. (2005). 'Practices and beliefs in mistake-handling actives: a video study of Italian and US mathemtaics lessons', *Teaching and Teacher Education*, 21*(5)*, pp. 491–508.

Shayer, M. (2003). 'Not just Piaget, not just Vygotsky, and certainly not Vygotsky as alternative to Piaget', *Learning and Instruction* 13*(5)*, pp. 465–85.

Skipper, Y. and Douglas, K. (2012). 'Is no praise good praise? Effects of positive feedback on children's and university students' responses to subsequent failures,. *British Journal of Educational Psychology*, 82*(2)*, pp. 327–39.

Slavin, R.E., Hurley, E.A. and Chamberlain, A. (2003). 'Cooperative learning and achievement' in W.M. Reynolds and G.J. Miller (Eds.), *Handbook of psychology*. Hoboken, NJ: John Wiley & Sons.

Soderstrom, N.C. and Bjork, R.A. (2015). 'Learning versus performacne: An integrative review', *Perspective Psychological Science,* 10*(2)*, pp. 176–99.

Steuer, G., Rosentritt-Brunn, G. and Dresel, M. (2013). 'Dealing with errors in mathematics classrooms: Structure and relevance of perceived error climate', *Contemporary Educational Psychology*, 38*(3)*, pp. 196–210.

Stigler, J.W. and Hiebert, J. (2009). *The teaching gap: Best ideas from the world's teachers for improving education in the classroom*. New York: Simon and Schuster.

Sweller, J. (1988). 'Cognitive load during problem solving: Effects on learning', *Cognitive Science,* 12*(2)*, pp. 257–85.

Sweller, J. (2016). 'Working memory, long-term memory, and instructional design', *Journal of Applied Research in Memory and Cognition, 5(4)*, pp. 360–67.

Tulis, M. (2013). 'Error management behavior in classrooms: Teachers' responses to student mistakes', *Teaching and Teacher Education, 33*, pp. 56–68.

Van-Dijk, D. and Kluger, A.N. (2000). 'Positive (negative) feedback: Encouragement or discouragement?' *15th Annual Convention of the Society for Industrial and Organizational Psychology*. New Orleans, LA.

Wallace, I. and Kirkman, L. (Eds.), (2017). *Best of the best: Progress.* Carmarthen, UK: Crown House Publishing.

Wiliam, D. (2006). 'Assessment for learning: why, what and how', edited transcript of a talk given at the Cambridge Assessment Network Conference on 15 September 2006 at the Faculty of Education, University of Cambridge.

Wiliam, D. (2011). *Embedded formative assessment*. Bloomington, IN: Solution Tree.

Wiliam, D. and Leahy, S. (2015). *Embedding formative assessment: Practical techniques for K-12 classrooms*. West Palm Beach, FL: Learning Sciences International.

Wiliam, D. and Thompson, M. (2006). 'Integrating assessment with learning: what will it take to make it work?' in C.A. Dwyer (Ed.), *The future of assessment: Shaping teaching and learning*. Mahwah, NJ: Lawrence Erlbaum Associates.

Woollett, K. and Maguire, E.A. (2012). 'Exploring anterograde associative memory in London taxi drivers', *Neuroreport, 23(15)*, p. 885.

Zierer, K. and Hattie, J. (2017). *10 mindframes for visible learning: Teaching for success*. Oxford, UK: Routledge.

Useful online resources

www.shirleyclarke-education.org for Shirley's streamed video platform.

Youcubed: www.youcubed.org for Jo Boaler's mathematics program.

www.mindsetworks.com for the growth mindset.

https://eleducation.org for Ron Berger's work.

YouTube for 'Austin's Butterfly' lesson with Ron Berger.

Index

Note: page reference in italics indicate figures.